THE DOG CARE MANUAL

THE
DOG
CARE
MANUAL
DAVID ALDERTON

BARRON'S

A Quarto Book

First U.S. edition 1986 by Barron's Educational Series, Inc.
Barron's Educational Series, Inc. has exclusive publication
rights in the English language in the U.S.A., its territories,
and possessions.

All inquiries should be addressed to:
Barron's Educational Series, Inc.
113 Crossways Park Drive
Woodbury, New York 11797

International Standard Book No: 0-8120-5764-3

This book was designed and produced by
Quarto Publishing Ltd.
The Old Brewery, 6 Blundell Street,
London N7 9BH

Senior editor Zuza Vrbova
Art editor Hazel Edington
Designer Ross George
Design assistant Ursula Dawson
Illustrators Craig Austin, Gill Elsbury, Vana Haggarty,
Val Hill
Art director Peter Laws
Editorial director Jim Miles

Typeset by Q.V. Typesetting Ltd and
Ampersand Communication Ltd, London
Paste-up by Mick Hill, Paul Gardner
Manufactured in Hong Kong by
Regent Publishing Services Ltd.
Printed by Leefung-Asco Printers Ltd, Hong Kong.

• With special thanks to Lynne Shippam

CONTENTS

TAMED DOGS

When wolf pups were first domesticated, 20,000 years ago, it was the first step in a long process that would provide humans with a loyal friend and helper. The dog's close relationship with man dates back thousands of years.

? **WHEN WERE DOGS FIRST DOMESTICATED?**

Archaeological evidence suggests that dogs had been domesticated by 10,000 BC; early remains have been found in present-day Denmark and West Germany. One of the most touching discoveries from this period was in Israel where a young puppy was found in a grave alongside the body of its owner. Indeed, the keeping of dogs appears to have developed quite rapidly, worldwide. Dogs were to be found in North America about 5,000 BC, having been introduced by the early settlers from Asia.

At first, domestic dogs appear to have been quite uniform in appearance and certainly lacked the exaggerated traits associated with various contemporary breeds. As civilization proceeded, however, dogs began to evolve to perform particular functions in the community. Some were used to work with stock, while others served as guards. The deliberate selective breeding of dogs to develop a particular physical type considered ideal for the breed concerned is a recent trend. It began about 150 years ago. Today, there are at least 300 different breeds worldwide; some are not kept for show purposes and remain localized in their distribution. As the evolution of the dog has proceeded, some breeds such as the Ban Dog have disappeared; new breeds will undoubtedly emerge.

? **WHAT SPECIES OF WILD DOG GAVE RISE TO THE DOMESTIC DOGS SEEN TODAY?**

Almost certainly, all of today's breeds are descended from the wolf, which formerly had a much wider distribution than today. Studies have

Domestic dogs are thought to have evolved from four basic wolf stocks that lived in different parts of the world, depicted as a family tree (*right*). The North American wolf is believed to be the ancestor of the Eskimo dog — even today these dogs still look much like wolves. The Chinese wolf is thought to be the ancestor of Chows, Toy Spaniels and the Pekingese breeds. The Indian wolf was probably the ancestor of a large group that includes Greyhounds and Salukis and the European wolf is thought to have given rise to Sheepdogs, Terriers and related breeds.

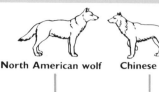
North American wolf   Chinese wolf

Eskimo dog   Chow

Pekingese

Jackals, such as this black-backed Jackal, *Canis mesomelas*, (*above, top*) may have been involved in the domestication of the dog but recent studies suggest that dogs are closer to wolves.

The Dingo (*above*), was a domesticated dog in Australia that reverted to the wild, although some are still found around human settlements.

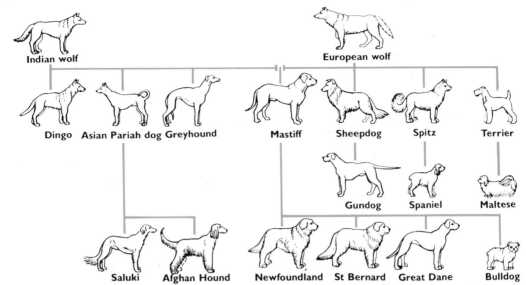

Indian wolf — Dingo — Asian Pariah dog — Greyhound

European wolf — Mastiff — Sheepdog — Spitz — Terrier

Gundog — Spaniel — Maltese

Saluki — Afghan Hound — Newfoundland — St Bernard — Great Dane — Bulldog

The Gray Wolf, *Canis lupus* (*left*) is thought to be the ancestor of the domestic dog. It is found in North America, Europe and Asia, showing considerable variation in both size and color across its extensive range.

revealed a close similarity between the skeletal structure of smaller wolves and the early domesticated dogs. Furthermore, detailed comparative behavioral studies have shown very close links between these two groups of canids. Differences occur solely in hunting routines, in which domestic dogs are not normally involved.

Some suggest that dogs could be descended from the Golden Jackal *(Canis aureus),* and superficially, this theory appears attractive. These jackals are scavengers; they often live close to human settlements and are relatively small in size. Yet serious behavioral and anatomical differences tend to eliminate this possibility. It has also been proposed that a wild canid, now extinct, might have been the direct ancestor of the domestic dog. There is no firm evidence available to support this view, however, and it now seems certain that the smaller races of wolf gave rise to the wide diversity of domestic dogs seen today. In fact, behavioral and instinctive traits, typical of our domesticated dogs can be traced back to pack hierarchy of wolves.

SECTION 1
UNDERSTANDING YOUR DOG

THE YOUNG DOG

1

Choosing a puppy can be difficult, especially when confronted with a number of young dogs. The first choice is between a pedigreed and a crossbred dog but, there are a number of other important factors that should be considered before actually setting out to obtain a dog. Subsequently, the settling-in phase and early training will be vital to integrate the puppy fully into its new environment, and should help to insure that it grows into a responsive and obedient adult dog. The playful natures of puppies make them wonderfully appealing, although mature dogs may be more suitable for some people, notably the older owner.

Puppies are always playful and sometimes quite disruptive (*right*) but they do like to integrate and become part of the family.

CHOOSING YOUR PUPPY

It is important to think very carefully before deciding to acquire a puppy. They are demanding animals and have to be trained to integrate fully into family life.

These Norfolk Terrier puppies will probably all grow up to be gentle and even-tempered dogs but it is wise not to select the most dominant nor the most submissive one of the litter. Ideally, your puppy should fall between these two extremes in temperament and be alert, curious and playful.

SHOULD I BE OBTAINING A DOG AT ALL?

Owning a dog can be a great source of pleasure as millions of people worldwide will testify, but not everyone is able to devote the time and care necessary to insure a dog's well-being. Keeping any pet places certain obvious restraints on the person involved in its care, and dogs rank among the most demanding of companion animals. A dog will need to be fed, exercised and groomed on a regular basis, and this is likely to take up at least an hour every day throughout the year. The cost of keeping a dog can prove a significant burden on finances too. There will be expenditure on food, equipment and routine veterinary care, and certain breeds may require professional grooming. Other incidental costs are boarding kennels and licensing.

Introducing a dog of any type into the home will inevitably cause some disturbance to the domestic routine, and it is certain to result in extra work. For example, all dogs shed dead hairs and they rapidly accumulate unless they are cleaned up daily. Some damage to the home or furnishings may also result from ownership of a dog, especially a puppy. This is more likely to happen if the animal is bored. As much time and attention must be given to a dog, as to an individual member of a family.

SHOULD I OBTAIN A MONGREL OR A PEDIGREED DOG?

A mongrel is a dog which belongs to no specific breed, whereas a pedigreed animal, as its name suggests, has been carefully bred over generations to conform as closely as possible to the prescribed standards for that particular breed as laid down by the appropriate authority in the country concerned. The likely adult size and shape of a young pedigreed dog can, therefore, be assessed with much greater accuracy than can that of a mongrel puppy. The feet can prove a useful indicator of the potential size of a young mongrel, however; relatively large feet compared with body size suggest that the puppy will develop into a big dog. By the age of four months, any dog, including a mongrel, should be about two-thirds of its final adult size.

Mongrels can often be obtained at little or no cost, but the purchase of a pedigreed dog is likely to prove an expensive undertaking, reflecting the time and care that has been expended on developing the bloodline. For those wishing to show their dog later in life, however, a pedigreed animal is clearly essential. It is often said that mongrels are less prone to illness than their pedigreed counterparts. While this is untrue in the case of infectious diseases, it is certainly correct that mongrels are less at risk from the inherited and congenital disorders that can afflict most pedigreed breeds.

SHOULD I OBTAIN AN ADULT DOG INSTEAD OF A PUPPY?

A young puppy is likely to prove more adaptable than an adult dog and is certainly preferable for a home with children. Older dogs can prove nervous, especially if they have had several homes previously, and they may not be used to children. They will take longer to settle into the domestic environment and are likely to be relatively unresponsive to training. Difficulties that can arise are, for example, the inability of the dog to respond to a new name and its initial reluctance to remain with its new owner when let off the leash. Given time and patience, however, such problems can be overcome to a great extent, but the settling-in period for an adult dog can be a difficult time, especially for the novice owner and particularly if the dog's origins are unknown.

If you intend to exhibit your dog later, you may want an older individual whose show potential can be assessed more easily than a puppy's. But a dog that has lived most of its life in a kennel will also have difficulty adapting to a domestic environment. Studies have shown that there is a so-called socialization period in the life of young dogs between the ages of about six and thirteen weeks during which time they need to be exposed to human company. The more attention they receive during this time the better they will settle in the home. A particular difficulty associated with dogs kept under kennel conditions during the early formative months of their life is that they have never been housetrained, and this can prove difficult to teach at a later stage.

? IS IT PREFERABLE TO BUY A DOG OF A PARTICULAR GENDER?

As a general rule, male dogs are more prone than females to escape and wander off, particularly in an area where there are a number of dogs and perhaps a bitch in heat nearby. They can also prove less responsive to training. For these reasons, bitches are preferred as guide dogs for the blind. The major drawback in owning a bitch, however, stems from the two periods of reproductive activity each year and the risk of an accidental mating during these "heats" leading to unwanted puppies. Another troublesome side effect can be the occurrence of phantom pregnancies.

Selecting a puppy from a private home means that you can meet the mother, note how the puppies behave among their littermates, and pick one out at your leisure. Puppies from a private home are usually well balanced, due to the benefits of good personal care and early contact with people.

DO DOGS DIFFER SIGNIFICANTLY IN TEMPERAMENT?

The various pedigreed breeds have been developed for specific purposes and thus do exhibit some variation in temperament. Nevertheless, there is obviously pressure for all breeds to be sociable in human company! The difference in temperament is perhaps not marked in the training sphere. Gundogs such as retrievers are relatively responsive to training compared with others such as the so-called sight hounds like the Afghan Hound, which have been developed for chasing game over considerable distance. Guard dogs such as the Rottweiler are often highly suspicious of strangers but generally tolerant of those they know well. Perhaps the least satisfactory group of dogs in terms of temperament for use as family pets are those bred specifically for fighting, such as the Staffordshire Bull Terrier. They can be easily provoked to bite by children as well as by other dogs; of course some individuals are more tolerant than others, and firm training can help to overcome such tendencies. Breeders have also made

The Komondor has an unusual coat (*above*) that consists of cords which must be separated if the coat becomes wet, to prevent matting. This breed also needs firm control and training.

The varying size of dogs is irrelevant to their compatability — a Great Dane can be seen in harmonious company with a Yorkshire Terrier (*left*). The various breeds have been evolved for different purposes, and their temperaments may vary somewhat as a result.

The bond between a child and a dog can become very strong, but in the first instance, the child must be taught not to tease or hurt the dog in any way. Mutual trust is important (*right*).

strenuous efforts to purge aggressive traits from contemporary bloodlines.

Nevertheless, temperamental disorders do occur and often receive widespread publicity, particularly in popular breeds such as the German Shepherd (formerly known as the Alsatian). Certain bloodlines exhibit neuroses more often than others, and it is a good idea to look into this by talking to breeders before obtaining a dog. Not only the large breeds can be affected; indeed, some smaller dogs may well exhibit such behavior. In the United States, the problem is well recognized in Bernese Mountain dogs and certain poodles. Always consult a local veterinarian for advice as soon as possible if a dog starts showing aggressive traits. Otherwise, serious injury may result.

ARE CERTAIN BREEDS MORE OF A LIABILITY IN THE HOME THAN OTHERS?

A large dog will need more space than a smaller one, and the bigger breeds, in their exuberance, may inflict accidental damage on the home by

knocking a cherished ornament off a low table with a sweep of the tail, for example. Some breeds such as the St Bernard have a tendency to drool saliva from their mouths, and this can be deposited on furniture or carpeting. The majority of dogs molt, and some hair, even with fastidious daily grooming, will be deposited around the home. There are certain breeds, however, including the Bedlington and Kerry Blue Terriers and poodles, which do not lose their hair in the conventional sense. They will need regular clipping and stripping to keep their coats trim and free of dead hair respectively. The flattened faces associated with the achrondoplastic breeds such as the Bulldog, Pug and Pekingese may lead to snuffling because of their compressed and shortened noses. This habit tends to worsen as the dog gets older and can become a source of irritation to some owners.

OUR CHILDREN SUFFER FROM ASTHMA. WILL IT BE SAFE TO BUY A PUPPY FOR THEM?

It would be sensible to seek medical advice first since allergies to dog hair and dust are certainly not unknown and may complicate an existing medical problem. Consider one of the breeds which do not shed in the conventional way or opt for one of the so-called "hairless" dogs such as the Chinese Crested. Unfortunately, this, like its Mexican counterpart, is a relatively scarce breed, and it also needs special protection during cold weather.

SHOULD WE GET A DOG WHILE THE CHILDREN ARE YOUNG?

The choice of a dog for a home where there are young children necessitates particular care. A dog of a fairly tolerant breed such as a Whippet or a Labrador Retriever is to be recommended. Small dogs are not always to be encouraged because they themselves may be injured if handled roughly and are more liable to bite as a result. In any event, always supervise contact between the children and the dog, particularly in the early stages when they are unfamiliar with each other. Children must be taught not to hurt the dog by playing roughly with it, and they should always be encouraged to participate in its care, even if only to offer the dog its food bowl. It is of course vital to follow a strict deworming schedule, as advised by your veterinarian, because of the slight risk of the transmission of parasitic worm eggs from dog to child. This is more likely to occur outdoors, and dog excrement should be removed from the environment on a daily basis.

MY WORK KEEPS ME FROM HOME ALL DAY. I WOULD LIKE A DOG, PARTLY TO DETER BURGLARS. WHAT BREED DO YOU SUGGEST?

Use the money you would have spent on a dog either to install a burglar alarm or to increase your insurance coverage. Dogs are social creatures by nature and should never be shut up all day without attention on a regular basis. Puppies in particular will prove highly destructive under such conditions and may well attract complaints from neighbors as they are likely to howl for attention. It will be virtually impossible to train a young dog kept in this way, and the inevitable soiling of carpets will be a source of constant frustration to you. Older dogs may be left occasionally for short periods, but be sure to encourage them to use the yard beforehand and always leave a fresh supply of drinking water available while you are away.

 MY ELDERLY MOTHER HAS ALWAYS HAD A DOG AND NOW WANTS ANOTHER AS A COMPANION. SHE LIVES ON HER OWN. WHAT DO YOU SUGGEST?

Studies being undertaken into the relationship between pets and their owners are confirming the importance of pet ownership, particularly for people living alone. As to whether your mother would be better suited to another type of pet such as a parakeet, the decision depends to a great extent on her physical health, and on the amount of assistance the family can offer her in caring for a dog. The type of dog should be considered very carefully. A puppy may prove too difficult, as would a large dog. Ideally, this is a situation where an older small dog, known to be of reliable temperament, would be ideal, but unfortunately a dog of this type is often difficult to find. Try to help with exercising, particularly during the winter months when pavements can be slippery. A dog could cause your mother to fall and hurt herself.

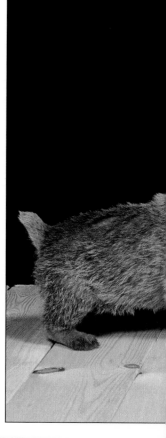 **WE ALREADY HAVE A CAT AND A DOG IN THE HOME AND HAVE BEEN OFFERED A YOUNG PUPPY BY A FRIEND. WILL THEY GET ALONG TOGETHER?**

Cats tend to ignore a new canine resident in the home, but this does not mean that the cat accepts the newcomer at once! The animals will need time to come to terms with each other. This stage must not be forced, but conflict must be avoided in the interim. The same applies when a new dog is

As companions for elderly people, dogs are ideal (*above*). But, the choice of dog needs to be considered carefully — obviously, a large, boisterous puppy would be unsuitable in many cases.

Puppies are inquisitive, and will naturally be interested in other pets, such as cats and so scenes such as this Norfolk Terrier playing with a tabby kitten are not unusual (*right*). Indeed, a strong bond can develop between a puppy and kitten as they grow up together.

An older dog may well appreciate the company of a young individual (*right*), although care must be taken during the early stages to insure that the established dog does not feel challenged by the newcomer. There are various ways of minimizing the risk of such conflict.

introduced alongside an established dog. Feed them separately so there is no risk of fighting over food, and reassure all concerned. Remember that the newcomer is invading the territory of the resident dog, particular reassurance needs to be given to the older dog so that it does not feel that its position as the dominant individual is being usurped by the newcomer. Hierarchy is important to dogs and invokes strong instinctive feelings that are derived from their ancestors — packs of wolves.

There is less likelihood of conflict when a puppy is introduced; an older dog may challenge the hierarchy. The rigid social structure existing within a pack of wild dogs serves to prevent serious conflict, and this arrangement still exists in their domestic counterparts. Keep favoring the established dog so there is less likelihood of a challenge from the new arrival, but remember that the temperaments of the individuals concerned will vary. It may be a good idea to introduce them first on neutral territory outside the confines of the home — in a nearby park, for example. Bitches as a rule tend to be less aggressive than male dogs, and they are more likely to live alongside each other in harmony than are two male dogs. The introduction of a younger companion to an older dog can encourage a more lively disposition in the existing pet once both are accustomed to playing with each other.

The **Afghan Hound** (*left*) is one of the most fashionable breeds to acquire but people do tend to overlook the fact that it is also one of the breeds that demands most attention. The Afghan's long, soft coat needs plenty of grooming, training them may be difficult and they need considerable exercise.

Animal Welfare Organizations (*right*) provide many delightful pets — both mongrel and pedigreed. Litters of puppies are frequently given to these organizations and if new homes are not found for them, the puppies may have to be destroyed.

WHICH IS THE BEST TIME OF YEAR TO OBTAIN A PUPPY?

In an ideal world, the best time is probably spring so that when inoculations are completed, the young dog can be trained out of doors at a time when the weather and day length are most favorable. Do not obtain a puppy in the summer if you are just going off on vacation, as this will disrupt the training routine. And most reputable kennels will be reluctant to take a young dog before it is fully protected by inoculations. It would also be extremely disturbing for a dog to be transferred to a new home and then moved again to a kennel within the space of a few weeks. Also, never buy a puppy at Christmas when the home is likely to be in disarray and full of visitors, as there will be little time to take care of the needs of the newcomer. It is no coincidence that most dogs are abandoned or discarded by their owners at these times of year.

ARE SOME BREEDS LIKELY TO NEED MORE CARE THAN OTHERS?

Certainly the long-haired breeds, such as the Afghan Hound, will need more attention by virtue of their coat type. This applies not only to grooming, but also to drying the coat after the dog has been out in the rain. And the long hair around the feet will attract mud. Certain light-colored dogs may require regular washing around the eyes where the tear fluid stains the coat. Apart from considerations of coat care, some smaller dogs can also prove fussy and faddish eaters, and this may necessitate additional care and be a source of worry to owners.

HOW DO I FIND A PUPPY OF A PARTICULAR BREED?

There are various ways. Attending shows can be particularly valuable if you are seeking a dog for exhibition purposes at a later date. You can see which bloodlines are winning regularly and also the type of dog preferred by the judges. Details of shows can be found in the various national dog periodicals. These may also carry advertisements from breeders offering surplus stock for sale. A puppy of a popular breed will not be too difficult to obtain, but one from a scarcer breed may involve a wait. In some countries, directories, produced and revised annually, give details on breeders and the breeds they have available. The American Kennel Club (AKC) will also be able to give you details. There are no recommended prices; generally, rare breeds and puppies from acclaimed bloodlines are relatively expensive. Occasionally, a breeder may have a poorly colored or marked puppy available at a substantially reduced price. Beware of any that have physical defects, since these may prove more expensive in the long term as veterinary fees mount up. Actually, a veterinarian may be able to suggest a reliable breeder in the neighborhood, providing the breed is not too rare.

? I'M NOT INTERESTED IN A PEDIGREED DOG. WHERE CAN I OBTAIN A PUPPY?

You could look at local advertisements in newspapers; they often offer both pedigreed and mongrel puppies. Alternatively, some pet stores do have puppies for sale, but check such dogs closely. Staff may not be as knowledgeable as a breeder, and the mixing of young dogs from various premises can present disease problems less likely to arise in a dog purchased directly from the breeder. This also applies to animal shelters or pounds which have a constant input of dogs. Some are unlikely to have been inoculated and could be incubating diseases such as distemper. Such organizations usually have a surplus of older dogs rather than puppies, but litters are brought in from time to time. Do not be surprised or offended if you are asked questions and visited at home before being given a dog from an animal welfare organization. It is simply doing its best to insure that the dog does not have to suffer the trauma of moving to another home for a short time and then being discarded again.

When a pedigreed dog is homed by such organizations, its pedigree documents are not usually handed over, to discourage breeding from the dog. Indeed, some organizations may even insist on a neutering agreement. The problem of unwanted dogs is now so great that many breed associations have established their own rescue groups for specific breeds, unlike the more traditional organizations which care for all unwanted dogs. Indeed pedigreed dogs are just as likely to end up homeless as mongrels. Those who try to home such dogs are invariably self-financed. Do not forget to give a donation to help their work continue. Hopefully, the public can be educated eventually to adopt a more responsible attitude.

I'M WORRIED ABOUT CHOOSING A PUPPY. CAN I BE GUIDED BY THE BREEDER'S ADVICE?

The vast majority of breeders are genuine, trustworthy people who are concerned that their dogs have a good home, and they will go to great lengths to advise a potential purchaser. Nevertheless, do not rely entirely on what you are told; look at the puppy and its surroundings. When making a preliminary telephone call to arrange a time to visit, it is possible to get an initial impression. Explain what you want and ask questions such as the price of the puppies for sale and whether breeding stock has been checked for inherited defects such as *hip dysplasia* and *progressive retinal atrophy*. A conscientious breeder will acknowledge your interest in the breed and arrange a convenient time for a visit. Always try to visit the premises, even if it means traveling a fair distance because traveling is preferable in the long term to receiving a puppy of the wrong type or one that is sick.

Breeders operating on a small scale frequently have litters of puppies living in the house. This insures that the young dogs are used to the domestic environment from birth — unlike those that have been reared in kennels. Individual puppies will vary in temperament; there is a distinct social order established almost from birth, and some are more dominant than others. These are usually first to the food, pushing their contemporaries out of the way. Young puppies will sleep for quite long periods, and such behavior is not necessarily associated with illness. Watch them for a short time before focusing on a particular individual.

POINTS TO CHECK

Are their surroundings clean? Any excrement evident on the floor should be relatively firm, unless they have been dewormed shortly beforehand. Healthy puppies are relatively fat, and when handled (with their owner's permission) they will have loose, pliable skin. Starting at the head, look at the eyes. These should be clear and free from any discharge which could stain the fur, particularly at the sides of the eyes nearest the nose. The nose should be moist in appearance, and the ears should appear clean. Moving down the body, look at the fur closely for any signs of fleas or lice. The ribs can be felt but should not be evident when the puppy is held.

Underneath, check that there is no swelling in the midline which might indicate an *umbilical hernia*. This, although not serious, might need to be corrected at a later date by surgery. The belly should not appear pot-shaped as this can indicate a heavy parasitic worm burden and shows a lack of care on the part of the breeder. The anal area should appear clean. Any swelling around the groin could be a sign of an *inguinal hernia*, which in this locality is more serious than in the umbilical position. Once back on the ground, the puppy

HIP DYSPLASIA

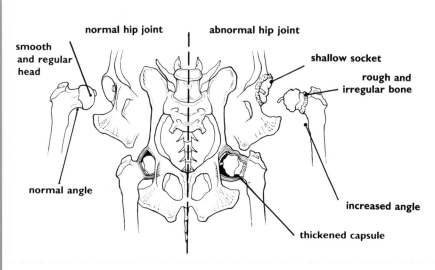

normal hip joint

smooth and regular head

normal angle

abnormal hip joint

shallow socket

rough and irregular bone

increased angle

thickened capsule

The hip joint is of the ball and socket type, with the head of the femur fitting into the socket of the pelvis. Hip dysplasia occurs when the development of the joint is faulty, or the socket is abnormally shallow. Radiography is used to screen breeding stock for this inherited problem, and also for diagnostic purposes.

SIGNS OF HEALTH

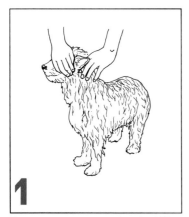

There are various points that should be checked before deciding upon a particular individual. The head should be examined for any evidence of lice (**1**). The eyes should appear clear of

any discharge, with no tear staining visible and the ears should be free from any unpleasant odor (**2**). Finally, with a puppy in particular, check that there is no trace of an umbilical hernia

(**3**). In addition to these physical indicators, the puppy should be active and alert.

should move nimbly, with no signs of lameness. It will also respond readily to noise, providing it is not deaf; this can be a particular weakness in dogs which have pure white coats, irrespective of breed.

If you are not happy with the puppies for any reason, do not purchase one. Remember, the puppy will become an integral part of your life for at least a decade; it is better to wait than to rush into an acquisition you will soon regret. A more thorough medical examination can be undertaken by your veterinarian when the puppy is taken for its inoculations. No reputable breeders are likely to want to sell a dog that is unsound, since this would be embarrassing and potentially damaging to their reputations and could also render them liable to legal action.

 WHAT QUESTIONS SHOULD I ASK THE BREEDER BEFORE TAKING MY PUPPY HOME? I'VE CHOSEN ONE FROM A LITTER, BUT IT ISN'T INDEPENDENT YET.
Prospective customers often view a litter of puppies before they are weaned. This enables the new owner to make preparations before taking the puppy home. Many breeders will provide you with

a diet sheet giving details of the food that the puppy has been eating. Always keep to this regimen for the first few days after picking up your puppy to minimize the risk of digestive upsets, and, for the same reason, carry out any changes to the diet gradually rather than suddenly. Check to see what inoculations the puppy has received, and if possible, get a certificate showing the date and type of inoculation that was administered. This can be of value to your veterinarian at a later date, particularly as there are now so many types of vaccine available and some differ in the protection they offer. It is also important to know how many times the puppy has been dewormed and the date of the last deworming.

In the case of pedigreed dogs, you should receive the appropriate documentation: the pedigree, setting out the ancestry of the puppy over the preceding generations, and either details of registration or a transfer card which must be returned to the appropriate authorities to notify them of a change of ownership. This is particularly important for dogs which may later be shown. The American Kennel Club is the final authority on what consitutes a breed, and if the dog is not registered as pure bred, it is called a mixed breed.

COMFORT FOR YOUR DOG

Settling a dog into a new environment calls for patience. Remember that the basic needs are the same as yours — somewhere clean and comfortable to eat, sleep and play.

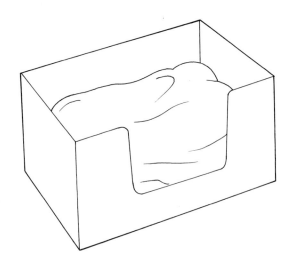

? WHAT EQUIPMENT SHOULD I BUY FOR OUR PUPPY?

There is a vast array of equipment now available, particularly in larger pet stores. For the puppy, however, it may be better to defer the purchase of some items, such as a permanent bed, until the dog is older and past the teething stage. Stainless steel feeding bowls are essential as they can be easily and thoroughly cleaned. For water, however, a ceramic bowl is preferable because it is heavier and less likely to be overturned. A knife and fork to prepare the dog's food may be useful; all the utensils used for the puppy should be kept separate from those used by the rest of the family.

A suitable bed can be made by cutting part of the front out of a large cardboard box with an open top and lining the inside with newspaper. The whole bed can easily be replaced if it gets soiled or is chewed. Around the bed, it is useful to have a suitable pen in which to confine the puppy when required. This will prevent it slipping out into the street, for example, when the door is open for any length of time. Pens of this type can be obtained from most larger pet stores. They usually consist of individual panels of standard size which clip together.

A light collar is to be recommended, even before the puppy is taken out of doors so it gets used to wearing one from an early age. Check that it fits properly; remember that the neck of the puppy grows with the rest of the body, and a collar should be adjusted accordingly. An identification medallion attached to the collar will insure that if the puppy escapes accidentally, it will carry its address and a telephone number. It can then be

Food and water containers must be easy to clean, durable and stable so that their contents are not easily spilled (*above, top*).

Identity tags are available in various forms. The capsule attached to this dog's collar (*above*) has full details of the dog's home included within, on a piece of paper. As an added precaution, these can be filled in, in indelible ink.

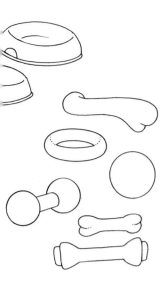

A bed for a young puppy is not essential, certainly until the teething phase has passed. Some owners then prefer to purchase beanbags for their dogs, rather than a conventional bed. If a bed is chosen, it will need to be easy to clean, and able to withstand the puppy's teeth (*far left*).

A wide variety of toys are commercially available (*left*). Generally, avoid the more elaborate types. Simple chews are popular with teething puppies.

returned without difficulty to its home. This information can be etched by an engraver on a metal disk or written with indelible ink (this latter method is less satisfactory). Or, a small capsule, with the details inside can be fitted to the collar. In various countries the law requires that dogs carry identification of this type.

Puppies especially are very playful; be sure that any toys you buy are not likely to be harmful. Always choose a large ball, for example, so that it cannot be swallowed accidentally. Rubber rings are useful for training purposes because they can be thrown for the dog to retrieve. These are unlikely to be harmful, but chewing should not be allowed. The young dog's desire to chew is quite natural and needs to be encouraged properly. Otherwise expensive shoes and furniture may be damaged irreparably by a puppy's teeth. Give the puppy a pair of old rubber slippers for the purpose, or buy one of the special chew toys that can be obtained from a pet store.

A playpen where the puppy can be confined for short periods is useful initially (*left*). The area should include a bed, as well as food and water pots. The puppy will soon come to recognize this as its own territory, and, having been out playing, will return to sleep here.

A vast range of equipment is currently available but only certain items are essential at first. The bed is an important aspect of a puppy's world and the puppy will soon learn to recognize it as part of its own territory. A clean cardboard box, with the front cut away for easy access, is the best option for the first few months, until the puppy has grown out of the chewing phase — otherwise it may chew up a brand new bed. The box should be lined with newspaper with a blanket on top, for warmth and insulation. Once the first milk teeth are lost and the chewing phase is over, the puppy can be provided with a permanent dog basket or a beanbag. Insure that the basket is easily washable, to prevent fleas and if you buy a beanbag, insure the outer covering is removable and washable. A special pen made from wire mesh panels which clip together can be useful to restrict the puppy at home or to use in the car as a traveling cage. Otherwise, a small

? WHAT OTHER EQUIPMENT DO I NEED FOR AN OLDER DOG?

A permanent bed is a good idea, but be sure it can be washed thoroughly. This will be necessary from time to time, especially when the dog is infested with fleas, because fleas will breed in the bed. Choose a bed large enough to accommodate the fully-grown dog. Wicker or plastic beds are widely available, but there has been a trend in recent years to dispense with a bed in favor of a beanbag. These are available in various sizes and are usually filled with polystyrene granules. They should have two coverings; the outer one should be removable and washable. A beanbag can also be a play area, but be sure that the covering is strong and cannot be ripped open accidentally. It is also safer to opt for one of the more expensive types with fire-retardant properties. Beanbags appear more comfortable than the traditional bed and are probably of value for dogs suffering from arthritic problems, because the dog is not restricted to a single position when resting on a beanbag as it is in a dog bed.

An appropriate leash (or lead), in conjunction with a collar, will be essential for walking the dog. A substantial leash should be acquired, particularly for a large dog. Leather is traditionally used in the design of leashes, but nylon is equally strong and can be scrubbed easily if it becomes soiled. Consider getting a harness if you own a Dachshund or any dog prone to neck problems as it will ease the tension in this sensitive area. An elderly person may find a harness helpful in picking a dog up because it can support the dog's weight. The only other equipment of this type that may be useful during the training phase is a choke (check) chain, but this is not always recommended and must be applied correctly if it is not to injure the dog. Never opt for an electric-shock type collar for training purposes. At best, these simply upset the dog; in fact, they are outlawed in certain countries.

Grooming equipment is mandatory for an older dog, and can be useful for a puppy to accustom it to this procedure from an early age. The tools required will depend to some extent on the coat of the dog concerned. Metal combs are available in various sizes, and some have handles which makes grooming a long-haired dog, in particular, easier.

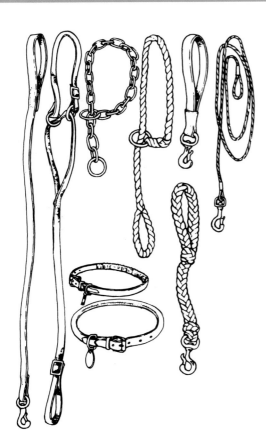

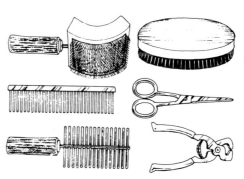

carrying cage is adequate for transporting your dog over short distances.

It is a good idea to buy a light, thin, adjustable leather or nylon collar and put it on your puppy around the home so that it will quickly become accustomed to wearing one. Broader collars are recommended for the larger breeds.

There is a vast array of toys currently on the market but the least elaborate, such as a large lightweight, plastic football and hide chews are preferable. An identity medallion is now a legal requirement in many countries, including the United States and the United Kingdom and there are several options available. The necessary grooming implements vary according to the kind of fur your dog has and apart from a soft brush are not essential at first (see p.54).

Plastic combs tend to break and are thus not advisable. While combs will remove some dead hair and help to prevent the coat from becoming matted, a stripping brush is recommended for the breeds that do not shed in the conventional sense. There are other brushes that can also be used for removing dead hair; they are made from either rubber or horsehair and are known as hand or grooming gloves because they fit over the hand. These are also used to polish the coat and give it an attractive luster. Another type of brush which fits over the hand by means of a strap is the dandy pad. It is often used on terriers and is thus sometimes called a terrier palm pad. In fact, the brush derived its name from the Dandie Dinmont Terrier, a small member of the Terrier group whose coat needs considerable brushing and care to look at its best.

When taking your dog out in the car, it is a good idea to restrain him behind a dog guard. Always choose a design with square or rectangular mesh rather than a series of bars. This is especially important for fine-nosed breeds such as the Whippet as they may get trapped in a barrier with bars. Dog guards do not necessarily have to be fitted to the structure of the vehicle. Simply attach them to the floor and roof by means of adjustable screw feet. If in doubt, consult your garage. With smaller dogs, it is possible to use an all-mesh carrying cage as an alternative to fitting a dog guard. These are more convenient and enable you to transport several dogs safely in a relatively confined space. Many exhibitors take several dogs by this means in the back of a station wagon, with the rear seats down, when traveling to and from shows.

Other essential equipment for the dog owner is a towel that can be used for drying the dog after a bath or when it has been raining. Dog coats are also to be recommended, especially during cold weather, for breeds such as the Italian Greyhound which feel the cold because they have only a thin covering of hair. Puppies will often do their best to remove coats, and a strong fastening on a coat of the appropriate size is essential. Some designs incorporate luminous material; this can be particularly useful in country areas because it alerts approaching car drivers to the presence of the dog and its owner on roads where there are no sidewalks.

New surroundings rapidly become familiar to a dog and he or she will soon settle in as part of the family (*left*). It will appreciate a beanbag both for sleeping and play purposes. Dogs should be kept out of bedrooms however, as apart from soiling and damaging the bedclothes, they can also introduce fleas to the bed itself.

 SHOULD I TAKE ANY SPECIAL PRECAUTIONS WHEN BRINGING MY PUPPY HOME?

Remember that this will be the first time the puppy is moved; it will not be accustomed to the unfamiliar sensation of traveling by road. It may be upset and could even be car sick as a result of the journey. If you intend to collect the puppy by car, try to persuade someone else to come with you, especially if you plan to bring the young dog home in a cardboard box lined with newspaper. It is not unknown for a puppy to escape from such confinement, and this could distract you at a dangerous moment.

When traveling on public transportation (pets are usually permitted on trains and buses, but find out in advance), remember that you may have to pay for the puppy and that the puppy should be contained securely, preferably in a carrying case or basket. If a cardboard case is used, remember to hold it from beneath even if it has a handle. Many cardboard carrying containers are quite flimsy and will weaken considerably when wet. It is not unusual for a puppy to urinate while in transit, and this could cause the bottom, and thus the puppy, to fall out. A thick layer of paper and a blanket should be placed on the floor of the carrying case, to absorb the urine and help the puppy to have a reasonably comfortable journey home. It is not recommended simply to carry the puppy because its sharp claws may cause you to drop it, and in any event, a young dog should be kept away from others until it has been fully inoculated.

WHAT IS THE BEST WAY TO SETTLE MY NEW PUPPY IN WHEN I GET HIM HOME?

Get everything prepared before you leave to collect it. Decide where you intend to keep your puppy and place its bed in this position. The place needs to be relatively warm and draft-free, and it should be quite easy to clean up after any accident bearing in mind that your puppy will not be housebroken. It is also important that the young dog should not be isolated but integrated as far as possible into the family. Many people decide to use the kitchen for this purpose, providing it is large enough! The kitchen is also usually near an outside door, and this will help with toilet training. Start by putting the puppy on a low tray on its arrival in case it wants to relieve itself. A cat litter tray filled with a suitable litter will suffice as a toilet when the puppy cannot go outside. After a few minutes, offer a small quantity of food and leave the puppy quietly to settle in. Feeding often stimulates defecation, so prepare for this by placing newspapers on the floor, especially close to the tray you have provided.

The first night in strange surroundings can be an upsetting experience for a young puppy. Do not be surprised if it howls for long periods at this time. Try to get it to settle down in its bed, but if all else fails, you may want to place it in a pen in your bedroom. Protect your rug as far as possible with a layer of plastic sheeting with a thick layer of newspapers on top. Never get angry with a young dog at this stage, even if it howls incessantly. This will simply upset it more than ever. Dogs are very sensitive animals and respond to the tone of your voice; it is much better to attempt to comfort the puppy by speaking in a soft, reassuring manner. The major problem with allowing the puppy to sleep in the bedroom is that it may refuse to sleep elsewhere in the house without considerable persuasion after it settles into its surroundings. When introducing strange dogs to each other, it is probably best to keep them apart at night at first in case both decide to sleep in the same place and disagree accordingly.

Try to establish a routine with set mealtimes for your puppy right from the start as this will be very reassuring. Follow the feeding directions provided by the previous owner as closely as possible at first. Decide upon the name for your pet and always use the name at every opportunity so that the puppy associates itself with this sound. If the whole family can be involved in the puppy's care from the start, so much the better because this overcomes any tendency for the young dog to develop into a "single person animal"

? MY NEW PUPPY LIKES TO SLEEP ON MY BED. IS THIS ALL RIGHT?

It is not really to be recommended for a number of reasons. For one thing, small puppies can grow into big dogs, and sharing a bed with an adult Great Dane could prove uncomfortable. Then there is the hygienic aspect. A puppy may lack control over its natural functions and soil the bed as a result. When the dog picks up fleas, as is virtually inevitable, these will be introduced to your bed and will in fact bite you. Flea bites can be intensely irritating and painful. Even intestinal parasites could be transferred to you from a dog sleeping in your bed. A certain amount of dirt and possibly other substances can also be deposited on the bedding especially in wet weather, and the characteristic odor associated with dogs may also be transferred to the bed. If you have difficulty persuading your puppy to settle in its own bed, try placing a hot water bottle filled with warm water under a blanket. The puppy probably cannot settle because it misses the warmth of its fellow litter mates; the gentle heat from the hot water bottle will be comforting.

? WHAT IS THE CORRECT WAY TO PICK UP A PUPPY?

Handle the puppy carefully and give adequate support from beneath so that the hindquarters do not hang down. You can carry a puppy resting in the crook of your arm with its hind legs being supported from beneath and its forelegs restrained by your other hand. It is useful to pick up a puppy regularly so that it will not be frightened when handled in this way later in life. Although a bitch may carry her pups when young by the scruff of the neck, do not follow this method as it can lead to injury in an older puppy and is uncomfortable. Methods of handling an older, larger dog will vary depending on its size.

PICKING UP A PUPPY

When picking up a puppy, be sure to provide adequate support for the hindquarters. This is most conveniently achieved by resting the dog, as shown, with the dog's feet being gently held by your hands. The puppy is less likely to struggle if firmly, yet gently restrained.

THE EARLY STAGES

Dogs, like babies, are creatures of routine, and like to establish a fixed pattern for mealtimes and other activities, that reassure them in their new home and lifestyle.

? WHAT SORT OF TRAINING WILL MY PUPPY NEED?

Training is often seen as a rather one-sided activity; that of imposing the owner's will on a dog. In fact, training can be valuable both to dog and owner. A dog that will stay on command is less likely than an untrained dog to dash wildly across the road into the path of oncoming traffic. It will not harass animals in a field when out for a walk and is thus unlikely to be shot by a farmer. Training also serves to emphasize the relationship between the parties involved. Dogs, being pack animals, look to their leader, and firm training, particularly of the more dominant breeds, will avoid behavioral problems later in life as the dog will recognize its subordinate role and not effectively challenge its owner's position. It is clear, therefore, that to get maximum enjoyment from dog ownership, you must train your dog well from the outset. Young dogs are most responsive to training; this can begin as soon as the puppy enters the home.

There are certain basic behavioral requirements that the dog must learn. It must obviously be housebroken and should be taught to ask to go outside when it wants to relieve itself. Within the home, it must learn not to damage furnishings or jump on beds. The young dog must respond to its name and allow items such as bones to be taken away without any form of resentment being shown. It must come to recognize other members of the family and show no aggression toward them or toward welcomed visitors.

Out of doors, the young dog must return when called, walk properly on a leash without pulling, and stay and sit when told to do so. It should not jump up on people, go into fields where there are other animals, especially sheep, or foul sidewalks. Overall, training will have been successful only if the dog responds without hesitation.

? WHAT BASIC TRAINING SHOULD I GIVE MY PUPPY?

Successful training depends to a large extent on repetition and praise when a command is carried out correctly. To start with, call the puppy by its name at mealtimes, and occasionally at other times of the day, rewarding it first with a piece of food when it comes. The young dog soon associates the sound of its name with either food or affection, and responds accordingly. Never tease the puppy with food if it fails to act as requested. This particularly applies to the command "sit." The sitting posture is a relatively natural position, and the puppy, having come on hearing its name, can then be encouraged to sit and stay while the food bowl is placed in front of it.

Strange dogs or newcomers should be fed separately, so there is no risk of fighting over food. Dogs are not usually fastidious about their food but when an individual is reluctant to eat, the presence of another dog may provide a stimulus.

SIT TRAINING

Initially, encourage your dog to sit, by pressing him firmly into a sitting position, using his name and the word "sit" simultaneously (**1**).

Eventually he will sit in response to an authoritative command only (**2**), especially if he is rewarded with a tidbit.

Always take the puppy outdoors into the yard, in good weather, or to a tray or box when the signs appear. Choose an area outside which will not become excessively muddy and is not part of the lawn, since the acidity in canine urine can kill grass over a period of time. If an accident does occur inside, there is no point in punishing the puppy unless it is actually caught in the act. It will not comprehend the reason for such treatment. Do not rub its nose in the spot concerned as this will serve no purpose and only be unpleasant. When the puppy is seen soiling a rug, speak to it harshly and smack it with the hand on its hindquarters firmly but not excessively hard. Never hit a dog around the head; this can cause physical injury and will encourage the dog to bite.

HOUSETRAINING

Initially, place the puppy outside first thing in the morning, last thing at night and after meals (**1**). Stay with him in the yard and encourage him to act in the appropriate manner, rewarding him if

he performs. Dogs will soon learn to relieve themselves in a particular spot and soon your dog will approach the door of his own accord, when the need arises (**2**).

The most important basic training during the early stages of the puppy's life is housebreaking. Dogs are naturally clean animals and do not soil their quarters as a general rule. They tend to relieve themselves in specific areas delineated by scent. This can lead to conflict in the domestic environment, however, because a puppy, having soiled a rug once, will then be attracted by its scent and return. It is therefore vital that an area that has been dirtied be left completely free of scent as well as being cleaned up thoroughly. Various preparations for this purpose are sold in pet stores. White vinegar is also useful, as is bleach on a suitable floor (being diluted as required). Accidents can be prevented by watching the puppy for the tell-tale signs, which are often apparent after a meal or when the young dog awakes. It will search for a suitable spot, sniffing the floor beforehand.

When training a dog, always be firm and consistent. This will give the best results because the dog will soon come to understand what it can and cannot do. Do not allow it to jump and sleep on chairs as a young dog, for example, and then attempt to prevent it clambering on the furniture when it has grown up. Try to be positive in your approach, encouraging your pet as far as possible, rather than scolding him if he fails to respond or disobeys. Dogs are usually keen to please their owners, and this trait should be uppermost in the trainer's mind. If a puppy starts jumping on you, place it firmly on the ground and say "no." After a short period, it will realize that such behavior is not permitted, and stop doing it.

? I REALIZE THAT I CAN'T TAKE MY PUPPY OUTSIDE INTO PUBLIC PLACES UNTIL IT HAS BEEN FULLY INOCULATED, BUT SHOULD I BEGIN LEASH TRAINING BEFOREHAND?

It is certainly useful to start such training early in life so that the puppy is used to walking on the leash before being taken out for the first time. Choose a suitable collar and leash and begin walking the dog up and down along a fence so that it is effectively sandwiched between you and the barrier. This will prevent the puppy pulling away and encourage it to walk in a straight line. The puppy may nevertheless try to pull ahead. If so, encourage it to adopt the correct position by stopping, saying "heel" and placing it in the correct position. These early sessions should be quite short, about ten minutes or so in length, and simply serve to get the puppy used to the restraining effect of the lead. Variations can also be introduced. Encourage the puppy to "sit" while on the leash, and to "stay", giving the commands clearly with the dog's name attached so it will learn to associate these commands with itself. Try to make training sessions fun for the dog. Do not get annoyed if it fails to respond immediately as it will probably be confused. Remember, that a happy dog will become a receptive, responsive and affectionate dog.

A well-trained Golden Retriever is patiently observing the rules of the road (*above*), as are the children with him. There is more chance of your puppy growing up to be as obedient and responsive as this if firm leash training is begun early in life.

HOLDING A LEASH

With your dog always on your left hand side, hold the leash with both hands, positioned at waist height. Never put your hand in the loop at the end of the leash or loop the leash around your hands as this may be dangerous if the dog tries to run away. Use your left hand for control, allowing the leash to slip through or jerking the leash, as necessary.

LEASH TRAINING

Walking to heel is taught by holding a light leash in your right hand, with the puppy always on your left hand side (**1**). If the puppy tries to pull ahead, call him and use an authoritative, consistent command such as "heel," and if he still continues to pull forward, jerk the lead firmly back (**2**).

Sit and stay training is the next stage. First, make your puppy sit in one spot and raise the leash above his head and circle round him slowly, repeating the "stay" command (**3**). To teach him to stay in this sit position, walk away, just a leash length, and if he does stay in the same position, return to him, giving plenty of praise. However, if he disobeys, physically return him to the original sitting spot, which will still be warm, and push him into the sit position, repeating the "stay" command (**4**), constantly until he learns to obey.

The recall is instilled into the puppy by calling his name, followed by a vocal "come" command, from the sit position, while still on the leash. If there is no response, or if he hesitates, simply jerk the leash simultaneously to your command (**5**). If he rushes up to you and jumps up, push him away, and encourage him back into the sit position (**6**).

Profuse praise at the end of each training session is an important part of the whole process and punishment is counter-productive. Also, remember that your puppy's powers of concentration will begin to wane after about ten minutes or so. Having learned these basic commands instantly, go on to teaching your puppy to respond in the same way without the leash.

I'M NOT SURE HOW TO CHOOSE MY VETERINARIAN. HOW SHOULD I SET ABOUT THIS?

If you are obtaining your puppy locally, the breeder concerned may recommend his own veterinarian. Or ask friends who have dogs whom they use. The other option is simply to choose the veterinary practice nearest to your home. This can be most convenient, particularly in an urban area where the practice is almost certainly going to have a "small animal" bias as distinct from veterinarians who treat mainly farmstock and horses, popularly regarded as "large animals." Since all veterinarians undergo comprehensive training, there is no need to worry about their competence with dogs, even if you have to call upon a large animal practice in an emergency. Nevertheless, the chances are that small animal clinicians will have more specialized equipment at their disposal, and this will save the need for a referral in some instances to another veterinarian. Veterinary hospitals may have additional facilities available, but all practices are able to hospitalize patients in their care, even if an initial consultation takes place at a branch office.

Always telephone ahead, if possible, to find out details of office hours, and make an appointment if required, making sure to tell the receptionist that you are a new client. Be sure to arrive promptly, and be tolerant if you are kept waiting. Emergencies do happen, and these can delay appointments in even the most efficient practices. An early check-up, at the time of the puppy's inoculation or before if you are concerned for any reason, is to be recommended. A veterinarian will be able to give your puppy a basic clinical examination and may turn up a problem that both you and the breeder were not aware of, such as a congenital heart defect. Although rare, a disorder of this type is clearly best detected early in life before later signs become apparent. It is also a useful time to ask any questions that are worrying you about your new pet. Do not hesitate to write them down beforehand; in the heat of the moment, they can be easily forgotten.

In the United States, medical insurance for animals is available, and some veterinarians have proposal forms available. Details can also be obtained via the various dog periodicals — usually in the advertisement columns. Considering the potentially high costs of treatment for a dog involved in a road traffic accident, it may well be worth taking out insurance. But, as always, read the small print carefully and pay particular attention to the various exclusions. Routine veterinary care, such as inoculations and neutering, are not covered. An added bonus of some schemes is that they also afford cover against third party claims, which must not be overlooked. The owner of the dog can be sued if, for example, the dog causes an accident or bites a visitor, and clearly, under certain circumstances, damages could be very high.

I AM CONCERNED ABOUT INOCULATIONS FOR MY PUPPY. WHAT VACCINES WILL IT NEED?

The vaccinations most often given are for *rabies, leptospirosis, distemper, infectious hepatitis, kennel cough* and *parvovirus*. These are all serious diseases, and the protection afforded by inoculation is highly recommended.

Many vaccines now available offer protection against a number of these diseases in a single injection. In the case of puppies, it is usual to give two injections at the ages of eight and twelve weeks followed by annual "boosters" to maintain immunity. This system follows the protection provided to puppies early in life by their mother's milk, specifically the portion known as *colostrum* which is produced for a short period immediately

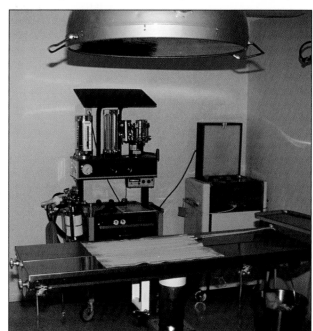

Practices now have a wide range of sophisticated equipment available to assist with the diagnosis and treatment of canine ailments.

Choosing a veterinarian will be essential shortly after you have acquired your puppy; mainly because preventative medicine is very important for dogs. The puppy will need a course of inoculations to protect against the major infectious diseases and your veterinarian will be able to advise you on any particular concerns about your puppy's health care at this time.

after the birth of the puppies. In the human child, protective antibodies against infections early in life are passed via the placental connection before birth. But this route is of very little significance in the dog, and antibodies are passed via the colostrum. These specific proteins are not digested but absorbed into the young dog's body.

As the puppy's own immune system starts to function to protect it from infection, so the level of the antibodies from the colostrum declines. In some cases, depending on the quantity of colostrum consumed by the individual puppies, the maternal antibodies may have disappeared before eight weeks of age, but this is generally the shortest time they will be effective. The protection afforded by the colostrum will have been lost in all cases by twelve weeks, but in certain specific instances, notably *parvovirus* in the Rottweiler, it can persist longer.

It is difficult to know precisely when the maternal antibodies have disappeared, and so, in the case of puppies which have contact with other dogs, as in a kennel, the first inoculation is given at eight weeks. This will then afford protection if there are no maternal antibodies left. Since antibodies will interfere with the action and efficacy of the vaccine, however, it is usual to reinoculate at twelve weeks, by which time the antibodies from the colostrum will have disappeared from the puppy's body. The vaccine can then stimulate the development of antibodies by the puppy's own immune system.

There are variations in this basic outline in the case of rabies inoculations, for example, so check with your veterinarian when you take your puppy in for a first check-up. A single injection given at eight weeks of age is not likely to offer full protection for the reasons given above, so be sure not to overlook the second set of inoculations. There are usually no side effects, and your puppy can be taken out for the first time in public places shortly afterwards.

DOGS' DENTITION

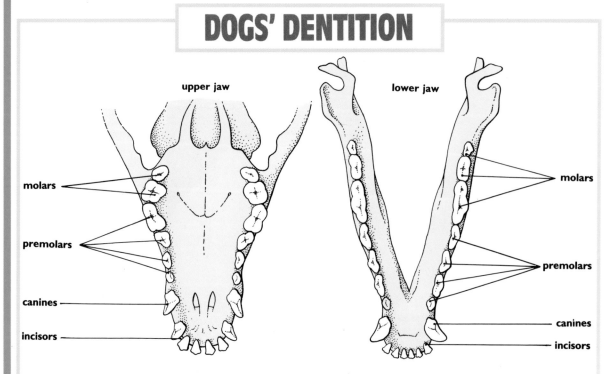

upper jaw

lower jaw

molars

premolars

canines

incisors

molars

premolars

canines

incisors

The jaw shape of dogs is quite variable, but the pattern of dentition tends to be constant. In breeds with narrow muzzles, there is a tendency for the incisors to become squashed together, whereas in broad-muzzled dogs like the Bulldog, there may be an undesirable gap between these teeth. The characteristic sharp and pointed canines are used for seizing and killing prey in wild dogs. They also assist in tearing meat into pieces, which tend to be swallowed whole rather than chewed. For this reason, dogs appear to bolt their food. This is quite usual behavior and need not be a cause for concern.

? MY PUPPY IS NOW SIX MONTHS OLD, AND CHEWING FEROCIOUSLY. HOW MUCH LONGER WILL IT BE BEFORE THE TEETHING PHASE IS PASSED?
Dogs have a full set of permanent teeth by the age of seven months, so you should be through the worst of it by now! The upper incisors are pushed out at about 14 weeks of age, as the permanent teeth erupt. The lower incisors are changed several weeks later, and the canines also at about 18 weeks. There are normally 28 deciduous teeth, and 42 permanent teeth. If you have a dog of one of the *brachycephalic* or "short-headed" breeds, such as the Bulldog, you may notice that the teeth are rather tightly spaced in the reduced dimensions of the jaw. In some dogs such as Chihuahuas the deciduous teeth are not always shed properly and may remain in the jaw alongside permanent teeth. If this appears to be the case, consult a veterinarian. He or she will be able to remove the deciduous teeth, under an anesthetic if necessary.

An uncontrollable urge to chew is typical of young puppies as their set of deciduous teeth are shed, and replaced by 42 permanent teeth. In order to divert the puppy from furniture and other household items, provide a toy (*above*) or a selection of "chews".

? I AM WORRIED ABOUT OVERFEEDING OUR YOUNG DOG. I FEED IT AS DIRECTED ON A CANNED DIET, BUT IT SCAVENGES, AND RECENTLY HAS HAD DIARRHEA AGAIN.

Young dogs do eat a relatively large amount for their sizes; their actual bodily requirements during this phase of growth can be as much as three times that of an adult dog of comparative size. There are special canned diets produced for young dogs which are enhanced to meet the increased demands of the body. The fact that your puppy scavenges and has a hearty appetite could be normal, or it may indicate a parasitic worm infestation. More details about this can be found later in the general health care section (see p.133). It is not unusual for puppies to occasionally develop loose stools, but this should not persist. Consult your veterinarian at once if you are worried, particularly if there is any blood in the stool.

Diarrhea need not be caused by an infection — a relatively common cause in dogs is an inability to digest the milk sugar known as lactose which ferments in the gut. The remedy in this instance is simply to withdraw milk from the diet. Always keep a watch on your dog's toilet activities. A blockage in the tract can create irregularities at the rear end. It is most likely to occur in puppies, they will chew and ingest virtually any substance that takes their fancy, if given the opportunity.

KINDS OF BITE

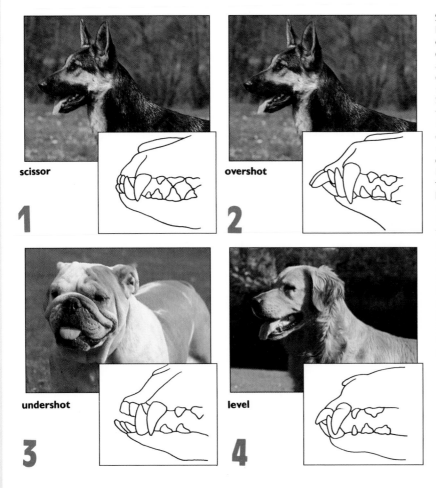

scissor

1

overshot

2

undershot

3

level

4

Selective breeding for looks has tended to emphasize differences in the arrangement of the upper and lower jaws and has resulted in much less effective jaws and teeth in some dogs. The German Shepherd Dog has been bred to ideally have a scissor-like bite (**1**) and a slightly longer, overshot jaw (**2**). An undershot jaw in this breed is considered a serious fault, leading to disqualification in the show ring. In the Bulldog, Pekingese and other short-faced breeds, the jaws have become so squashed that there may be no room for some of the teeth and the bite is referred to as undershot (**3**). In fact, some Bulldogs cannot hunt at all because their bite has become so distorted. The show standard for the Golden Retriever demands a level bite (**4**). Clearly, any pronounced abnormalities can give rise to difficulty in eating.

THE ADULT DOG

2

The daily care of a dog is straightforward, although initially, it may be difficult to decide between the wide array of foods and other equipment that are available today. Soon however, a routine will develop, covering all aspects of the dog's care, ranging from feeding and grooming to exercise requirements. Dogs have adaptable natures, but usually prove creatures of habit, preferring set daily schedules. They will soon come to identify mealtimes, and the time of day when they can expect to be taken for a walk. Some variation, within reason, is to be recommended however, otherwise the owner can become a slave to their pet!

Dogs reciprocate care and love accepting their owners as masters and companions and this attitude can be attributed to their wolf ancestry — dogs like to integrate into a human family as if it were their own pack (*right*).

FEEDING

Today it is easier than ever before to offer dogs a sound, balanced diet. The adverse effects of nutritional excesses, not deficiencies are most commonly seen — obesity and over-supplement of vitamins being increasing problems.

Ice creams or sweets are of no nutritional value (*right*) and will probably lead to tooth decay; also, excessive sugar may well result in diarrhea.

Various options now exist for feeding dogs, and recently, dry and semi-moist commercially produced foods have gained in popularity, at the expense of canned rations (*below*). These are complete foods, offering all the essential nutrients that a dog requires, although some canned diets are comprised of meat only.

? SINCE DOGS ARE CARNIVORES, SHOULD THEY BE FED ON MEAT ONLY?

No. In fact, dogs are less dependent on meat as the basis of their diet than cats are. A wide range of foods will keep your dog in good health; the main ingredients are the same as those which should be present in a human diet. Protein, comprised of various individual amino acids can be derived from either plant or animal sources. The protein of plants lacks certain so-called essential amino acids, which should be present in the diet if a deficiency is not to occur. Protein is necessary for growth, and has other specific functions, including a vital role in the cell membrane of the body. The healing of tissues also requires protein.

Carbohydrates in the diet are used essentially to meet the body's energy requirement, and are frequently provided in the form of biscuit meal, rice or bread. These ingredients of the diet are relatively cheap and are often used to bulk up a ration. The third major category of foodstuffs is fat, a highly concentrated energy source. Indeed, surplus carbohydrate is stored in the body as fat, and can be broken down later for use as an insulator against the cold, and to protect the vital organs such as the kidneys from trauma. There is an essential fatty acid, known as *linoleic acid*, which must be included in the dog's diet.

Vitamins, minerals and trace elements, although only required in minute amounts, are vital to the well-being of your dog. Vitamin D for example, controls the calcium stores of the body, and this mineral in conjunction with phosphorus is essential for a healthy skeletal structure.

? IS IT POSSIBLE FOR US TO MAINTAIN OUR DOG ON A VEGETARIAN DIET?

It certainly is feasible but will require extra work, and your efforts may not be appreciated by the dog, especially if it has been used to a meat-based diet. It may be possible to wean a puppy on to it successfully, but it will certainly be harder with an adult dog. Since plant protein is not as balanced in terms of its amino acid content as meat, opt for soya protein, which is the best form available. Unfortunately, amounts above 1 ounce per 12 pounds of the dog's weight tend to cause diarrhea. The carbohydrate content of the diet is easy to provide, but fat can be more of a problem. Eggs and high-fat cheese will be necessary, along with corn oil to act as a source of linoleic acid. Vitamins and minerals can be provided by way of a suitable preparation sprinkled over the food, and specific food items, such as carrots, can be used as additional sources on a regular basis. Apart from being more time-consuming, it may also prove more expensive to feed a dog on a vegetarian diet. While this may appeal to you, it is probably not in the dog's best interests.

FEEDING GUIDE FOR ADULT DOGS

	Toy Breeds less than 10 lb (for example Yorkshire Terrier, Toy Poodle, Chihuahua)	Small Breeds 10-20 lb (for example West Highland Terrier, Beagle, Cavalier King Charles Spaniel)	Medium Breeds 20-50 lb (for example Airedale Terrier, Basset Hound, English Springer Spaniel)	Large Breeds 50-75 lb (for example German Shepherd Dog, Labrador, Irish/ English Setter)	Giant Breeds 74-140 lb (for example Great Dane, Irish Wolfhound, Newfoundland)
Approximate daily calorie needs	2,000-4,000	4,000-7,000	7,000-14,000	14,000-19,000	19,000-30,000
Canned dog food (14 ounce cans) with mixer biscuit, fed in proportions of 2 : 1 by volume	$\frac{1}{4}$-$\frac{1}{2}$ can	$\frac{1}{2}$-1 can	1-1$\frac{1}{2}$ cans	1$\frac{1}{2}$-2$\frac{1}{2}$ cans	2$\frac{1}{2}$-3$\frac{1}{2}$ cans
Semi-moist dog food	4-4$\frac{1}{2}$ ounces	4$\frac{1}{2}$-8 ounces	8-15 ounces	15-21 ounces	21-33 ounces
Dry dog food	2-3$\frac{1}{2}$ ounces	3$\frac{1}{2}$-6$\frac{1}{2}$ ounces	6$\frac{1}{2}$-13$\frac{1}{2}$ ounces	13$\frac{1}{2}$-18$\frac{1}{2}$ ounces	18$\frac{1}{2}$-29 ounces

The feeding chart above, is simply a guide since food intake varies according to the level of activity and physiological state of individual dogs.

? **MY MOTHER IS CONVINCED THAT DOGS DO BETTER WHEN FED HOME MADE RATHER THAN COMMERCIALLY PREPARED FOODS. IS SHE RIGHT?**

Generally no, and indeed, the reverse could be true. The major problem with preparing a dog's diet oneself is making sure that it is suitably balanced, with adequate variety present. Indeed, feeding prime steak over a period of time will be harmful since it is low in vitamins A, D and E, and the calcium phosphorus ratio is seriously imbalanced. Coupled with a deficiency of vitamin D, this could give rise to skeletal abnormalities. The high protein level of such a diet would also be a waste of money, since the protein would be broken down to provide energy when there are much cheaper alternative sources, such as potatoes, available. It could also prove harmful in a dog that was already affected with kidney failure.

Various meats sold cheaply by butchers for pet food includes lungs and spleens, as well as tripe. All are valuable sources of protein, but the latter, being the stomach of ruminants, smells highly unpleasant unless "dressed". Ground meat invariably has a high fat content, especially if sold specifically for pets. In order to provide a balanced diet, the meat component should be mixed with a suitable biscuit meal or dog biscuits. Check that the brand you use is supplemented with the vitamins and minerals likely to be low in the meat content of the diet. It may be necessary, particularly for dogs with sensitive teeth, to soak the biscuits for a few minutes before feeding in order to make them more palatable.

? **SHOULD SUCH MEATS BE COOKED BEFORE FEEDING?**

Yes, it is highly recommended that you cook all such foodstuffs if they are purchased raw, to minimize the risk of disease to your dog. There are several parasites that can be transmitted via raw meat, including *Toxoplasma gondii*, as well as bacteria such as *Salmonella*, which is a frequent contaminant of raw poultry carcasses. Cooking also serves to improve the palatability of the food — boiled potatoes for example, are readily eaten by dogs while their raw counterparts are not. It may also be easier to feed a particular item once it has been cooked — eggs are a case in point, and hard-boiled eggs are a valuable source of protein. A fussy eater can often be persuaded to take warm food which has been cooked previously and allowed to cool; cold food is less popular. Should

your dog eat some raw meat by accident, it may have a digestive upset, but it will not become vicious, as some people suggest.

Any frozen or refrigerated foods should be allowed to warm up before being fed to your dog; otherwise they may cause a digestive disturbance. It is possible to cook a relatively large quantity of meats for example and deep-freeze them, weighing and packing them as required into plastic bags. By this means, a full week's meals can be prepared individually at one time, and you can simply take

the packs out of the freezer each evening for feeding on the following day after thawing out at room temperature overnight.

 I WANT TO FEED MY DOG A COMMERCIALLY PREPARED DIET. WHAT TYPES ARE AVAILABLE?

The huge size of the market for prepared pet foods means that manufacturers have spent a great deal of money researching in this area, not only to provide truly balanced convenience diets, but also to ensure that pet foods are as palatable as possible for the dogs themselves. It is not only easier, but also safer to use a complete diet because these eliminate the risk of nutritional deficiencies.

The canned diets are the main prepared food on the market at present. It is a complete food that meets all of your dog's nutritional requirements. It contains a mixture of muscle meat, stomach, heart, liver, lung, vegetable matter, vitamins and minerals. Some canned foods have a higher level of carbohydrate than others. For foods with the lower carbohydrate level, add one part cereal flakes, cooked rice or corn meal to two parts canned food. The cans can be stored for long periods of time without deteriorating, but when opened, they should be kept in a refrigerator and used as soon as possible. There is some evidence to suggest that the unused contents of a can should be transferred to a plastic container and the can itself discarded because of the oxidization of the interior of the can when it is exposed to air. The price of canned diets is variable, and is usually a reflection of the amount of carbohydrate present — this reduces the cost. The use of a corn meal with a canned food is a good idea in the case of the more expensive cans that have a higher level of meat. It is false economy to use protein as an energy source. Always follow the manufacturer's recommended feeding directions — the amounts suggested are likely to be on the generous side in any event. The excessive use of dog biscuits or corn meal is certainly to be discouraged as this will lead to obesity, particularly in a dog that is not working. Various specialized lines of canned foods can now be found on the shelves of supermarkets and pet stores for puppies and for the more fussy eaters. In the latter instance, however, cat food may prove a cheaper alternative. It has a higher protein content than dog food, as a general rule, and this can increase its palatability. A few canned dog foods may not be complete, but contain only meat of a particular type. If in any doubt, check the ingredients shown on the label.

The storage of dog food will vary according to its ingredients. Fresh items need to be kept refrigerated, and if deep-frozen for any reason, they must be allowed to thaw and warm up before being fed to your dog. Canned items, once opened must also be kept refrigerated. Foil packaging maintains a product's freshness and so, although there is no need to store them in a refrigerator, such items should be used up as soon as possible, after the package has been opened. Dried foods, with a very low water content, can be kept for a considerable period of time, although the vitamin content will decline, and the product should be used by the date recommended on its packaging. Once water or other fluid is added to a dried ration, it should then be treated as fresh food, and disposed of within a day, if not eaten.

Recently, the market for semi-moist dog foods has been expanding. Although designed to resemble succulent chunks of meat, these foods often contain relatively high levels of soya and have a lower water content, about 25 percent, compared with their canned rivals. They are usually sold in foil-wrapped sachets packed in boxes, and they may feature other ingredients, such as sucrose, which serve to preserve the food and improve palatability. Bear this in mind if your dog is diabetic.

Dried dog foods contain only about 10 percent water. There are various types of dried food, such as flakes, meal, pellets and expanded chunks. They can be kept without refrigeration and, unlike other foods, will not sour if left dry in a bowl for several days. Most manufacturers recommend immersing the dry food in water or even gravy at first to encourage the dog to take this unfamiliar foodstuff. If you follow this procedure, remember that the food, once moistened, will sour rapidly. Since dogs normally obtain a proportion of their fluid requirement from their food, a dry diet will encourage an increased water intake compared with a diet based on canned food.

? HOW DO I DECIDE HOW MUCH FOOD I SHOULD GIVE MY DOG?

Feeding directions accompany the convenience diets. Less dried food is required because it contains a reduced amount of water. As a general

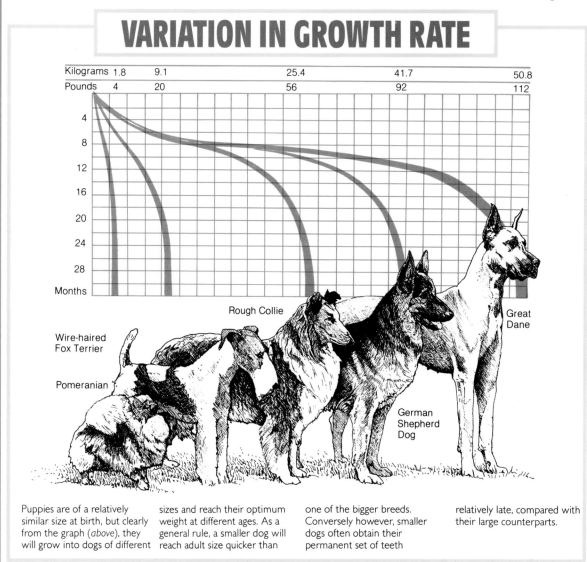

VARIATION IN GROWTH RATE

| Kilograms | 1.8 | 9.1 | 25.4 | 41.7 | 50.8 |
| Pounds | 4 | 20 | 56 | 92 | 112 |

Rough Collie

Great Dane

Wire-haired Fox Terrier

Pomeranian

German Shepherd Dog

Puppies are of a relatively similar size at birth, but clearly from the graph (*above*), they will grow into dogs of different sizes and reach their optimum weight at different ages. As a general rule, a smaller dog will reach adult size quicker than one of the bigger breeds. Conversely however, smaller dogs often obtain their permanent set of teeth relatively late, compared with their large counterparts.

rule, only 1 ounce of dry food is required for every 2.2 pounds of the dog's weight, whereas 3.5 ounces of a complete canned food will be necessary for the same dog. Smaller dogs tend to eat relatively more than their large counterparts because food requirement is more a reflection of surface area than of body weight.

There are various other factors involved in assessing the dog's nutritional requirement. The level of activity of the individual will have a bearing on its feeding needs: a working dog needs more food than a pet dog. Age is also significant; older dogs tend to need less food. In the latter stages of pregnancy, a bitch's appetite will increase considerably. Puppies, not surprisingly, also have a relatively high feed requirement to support their rate of growth.

It is hardest to estimate the amount of home-cooked meat and biscuit that should be provided since there will be no obvious guidelines available. Mix the biscuit on an equal weight basis with the cooked meat and feed 1 ounce per 2 pounds of body weight for a dog of average size.

? I AM WORRIED THAT MY DOG MAY BE BECOMING OVERWEIGHT. HOW CAN I CHECK THIS?

Weigh your dog on a regular basis and keep a note of the figures so you can see if it is gaining weight. With a small or medium-sized dog, the simplest way is to lift it up and stand holding it in your arms on a bathroom scale. Then weigh yourself and subtract this from the previous figure. Larger dogs can be more of a problem unless they can be coaxed onto the scale. The correct weight for a pedigreed dog can be found in many instances by referring to the breed standard where the ideal weight will be specified. In certain cases, two figures are given, with bitches usually being lighter than their male counterparts. Breeds vary considerably in weight; Pomeranians can be as light as 4 pounds, while Mastiffs may tip the scales at 190 pounds.

? HOW MANY MEALS A DAY SHOULD I GIVE MY DOG?

Follow the breeder's instructions at first with a puppy, which needs more frequent feeding than an adult dog. By the age of about nine months, most dogs are receiving either one large meal, usually in the early evening, or two smaller meals given morning and evening. This latter regimen is most applicable to smaller dogs. The main point, however, is to develop a system that suits you, as well as the dog. Do not, for example, feed the dog at

WEIGHT WATCHING

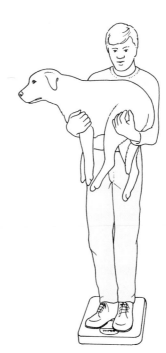

The easiest way to weigh a dog is to use an ordinary set of bathroom scales. Stand on the scales, holding the dog, and then subtract your known weight from the final figure shown on the scales — the result is your dog's weight. Apart from noting any trend towards obesity, regular weighing may help to detect chronic illness reflected by a loss in weight. Clearly, the dog must be used to being picked up. Some individuals may sit contentedly on the scales, but this is perhaps not very hygienic.

noon for several weeks and then suddenly change the time significantly as this will upset your pet. Dogs are essentially creatures of habit; they should receive their full daily ration at fixed mealtimes every day as far as possible.

In the United States, it is fairly common practice to leave the dog with food throughout the day so that it can help itself. Only dry food should be offered in this way, since meat products will tend to sour, bacteria will develop rapidly, and flies are likely to be attracted, especially during the warmer months of the year. Studies have revealed that dogs transferred to this system may eat more than usual at first, but the vast majority then tend to regulate their food intake in accordance with their energy expenditure so they do not put on excessive weight.

Under normal circumstances, with canned food for example, dogs will bolt their meal down within minutes of it being provided. This is quite normal behavior and need not be a cause for concern. Occasionally a dog, particularly a bitch with puppies, will vomit the food back up almost immediately. In the wild, a bitch will start to feed her offspring by this means, although such behavior may appear unsavory. The feeding routine during pregnancy and, subsequently,

during the rearing phase will need to be altered (see p.86). By the age of five months, most puppies should be receiving two, possibly three meals a day. It is inadvisable to put them on the free-feeding system described above, until they are nearly adult.

There is absolutely no benefit to be gained by starving a dog for one day a week. This idea comes from the behavior of wild dogs — they undergo periods of fasting when they cannot make a kill. In the domestic dog however, such action is more likely to encourage vices, such as stealing food, and possibly aggression towards members of the family.

? IS IT ACCEPTABLE TO FEED OUR DOG TABLE SCRAPS?

Yes, in moderation, but avoid feeding it while you are actually eating. It may not be easy to stop your children from doing this, however, but you must try. Otherwise, dogs soon learn to expect food when other members of the family are eating. In addition to encouraging obesity over a period of time, this will cause the dog to pester everyone and even howl if it is ignored. A dog that is not fed from the table is unlikely to develop these undesirable traits and will leave its owners to enjoy their meal without a battle of wills taking place.

Eating rapidly is fairly typical of most dogs (*left*) and loss of appetite can be an early sign of illness. Certain individuals do prove fussy eaters however, and may need to be coaxed to eat their food.

Feeding tidbits (*right*) should be avoided as this will lead to obesity over a period of time. In addition, if dogs are fed from the table, they tend to pester the family and guests at mealtimes relentlessly, awaiting scraps, which can prove very troublesome.

Dogs will eat a wide range of typical human foods — some will even eat fruit, especially apples. Avoid any hot spicy foods or excessively fatty items. Green vegetables will also be consumed by dogs, but tend to cause flatulence. Potatoes should be cooked as the starch will otherwise be fairly indigestible. Dogs can eat either brown or white bread, and loaves with extra fiber are perhaps beneficial. Some owners add a small amount of bran to their dog's diet to increase the level of fiber.

SHOULD I BUY A VITAMIN AND MINERAL SUPPLEMENT FOR MY DOG?

This depends to some extent on what you are feeding; in the case of a home-prepared diet, it may be advisable, especially if you are not using a corn meal with essential chemicals added during manufacture. Today, such is the craze for vitamins and minerals, however, that instead of showing signs of deficiency, dogs are now afflicted with problems resulting from overdosage with these chemicals. It is certainly not true in this case that if a little is good, a lot must be better. Always follow the directions given on the package. The young, growing dog is most at risk from excessive supplementation, and large breeds are the most susceptible since they normally develop more slowly than small breeds. Various abnormalities in the growth of their skeletal system and possibly other symptoms such as lameness will result.

On a balanced diet, it is unlikely that supplementation will be necessary, although under certain circumstances, it may be recommended. A dog with kidney failure, for example, may need a vitamin B supplement because excessive levels of this group of vitamins may be lost from its body. Perhaps one in a thousand dogs is incapable of making its own vitamin C, and specific supplementation to prevent scurvy from developing will be essential. This can be achieved by adding a tablet to its food. Allow 1 gram for a dog weighing 55 pounds. This vitamin deteriorates rapidly; do not purchase a large quantity and always keep it stored in the dark.

A shortage of vitamin D is unlikely because this vitamin is made by the action of sunlight falling on the dog's coat. It is stored in the liver along with the other so-called fat-soluble vitamins, A, E and K. There are specific instances when a vitamin K deficiency could occur, notably as a result of certain types of poisoning or excessive antibiotic therapy.

FEEDING BEHAVIOR

Dogs can prove great scavangers and will also thieve food, intended for human consumption. A combination of firm training and thoughtfulness will prevent conflict.

Performing tricks such as standing on hind legs (*above*), in return for tidbits should be discouraged as food between meals may spoil your dog's appetite and may eventually lead to obesity.

? DOES A DOG BECOME BORED BY BEING FED THE SAME FOOD EACH DAY? MY DOG TENDS TO BE A RATHER FUSSY EATER.

There is no convincing evidence to confirm that dogs get bored when given the same food every day. Provided they are receiving a balanced diet, there is no need to be concerned. By all means, vary the diet somewhat if you wish; offer cooked meat and corn meal occasionally instead of a convenience food. There is unlikely to be a link between the food you are offering and the dog's fussy eating habits. The root of the problem is almost certainly elsewhere. Do you feed a lot of tidbits between meals? This can depress appetite, particularly if the meal is less palatable than the snacks, although more nutritious. Do you get very concerned if your pet refuses to eat a meal? Some dogs soon come to realize that self-deprivation can bring rewards from their owners, either in the form of extra affection or more appealing food. Such behavior is most often seen in the toy (small) breeds.

Try to be firm. Cut out all additional food of any type offered between meals. Leave the dish of food available for an hour in the usual spot where the dog is fed, and then remove it even if none has been eaten. Repeat this procedure at the next meal time. The dog will soon come to recognize that it must eat what is being offered. It will not starve to death, even if it eats nothing for a couple of days. Do make sure that the food you are providing is as appealing as possible. You could add a little margarine over the surface of canned food, soak corn meal in warm gravy and make sure that the dog will not be disturbed more than necessary while the food is available. You may want to encourage him to eat by offering food on your hand.

A number of medical reasons exist for loss of appetite. If the dog suddenly refuses to eat and shows other symptoms, such as a lack of interest in other activities like going out, then it is advisable to contact a veterinarian without delay. Or if your dog plays with the food, particularly corn meal, it may have a painful tooth or gum infection. Studies suggest that male dogs tend to be fussier about their food than bitches. This may be a throwback to their wild ancestry, when the dominant male in a pack had preference at the kill.

? CAN I OFFER MY DOG CHOCOLATE DROPS?

Chocolate is very palatable to dogs and can be given occasionally. It is available in the form of special treats at some pet stores. Do not give large quantities. This may affect the dog's appetite in the short-term and can result in other problems such as dental decay, obesity and possibly *diabetes mellitus.* Excessive amounts of chocolate can also give rise to diarrhea, so always take care to place boxes of sweets well out of a dog's eager reach.

There are other, healthier tidbits that can be used as rewards during training and at other times. Raw carrots cut into small pieces appeal to many dogs to the extent in some cases that they may attempt to dig up carrots growing in a garden once they acquire a taste for them. Yeast tablets are also very palatable to dogs and provide a source of vitamin B. Always restrict the amounts of such items that you give, so the dog does not come to view them as an extension to meals rather than a reward for good behavior.

? SHOULD I LET MY DOG CHEW BONES?

From a strictly nutritional viewpoint, there is probably no need to provide bones, providing your dog is being fed correctly. Yet dogs certainly enjoy having bones to gnaw, and this activity may help to keep the teeth clean. There are potential dangers however; some dogs become extremely possessive about bones and need to be trained to relinquish them readily when told to do so. This can be carried out more easily with a young dog. Be careful when dealing with a strange dog as you cannot be sure how it will react. Provide only large marrow bones which cannot be accidentally swallowed causing a possible obstruction in the digestive tract. Chicken and rabbit bones, being light, are particularly dangerous; they splinter readily, often in the mouth where they can become embedded in the tissue. Larger bones such as those from chops may be inadvertently swallowed and become stuck in the throat. Try to be sure that the edge of the bones you provide are not rough, as fragments may break off and cause problems.

If, in the light of the above, you feel it is too risky to provide a bone for your dog to chew, consider one of the chew toys available at most pet stores.

Chewing bones is an enjoyable activity for dogs (*right*) but, from a dietary standpoint, they are not strictly necessary, although they may help to keep a dog's teeth clean. Some dogs do get very possessive about bones, and so they must be trained from an early age to relinquish them on command. In warm weather bones attract flies, particularly if there is any flesh still adherent and so dog chews sold in pet stores are preferable.

A **healthy dog**, in this case a cross-bred Cavalier King Charles Spaniel, crossed with a Whippet, (*right*) is totally dependent on his owner to provide food regularly which is of good nutritional quality, combined with plenty of exercise.

Eating grass is fairly common in dogs — it may act as a natural emetic or add fiber to the diet (*below*).

MY DOG IS A PERSISTENT SCAVENGER. WHAT IS THE REASON FOR THIS BEHAVIOR, AND HOW CAN I PREVENT IT?

Unfortunately, all dogs, to a greater or lesser extent, are scavengers by nature and will steal food if a suitable item presents itself. In certain instances, they may be driven by a medical reason. Pancreatic insufficiency, for example, often causes an increase in appetite; the dog will steal food at every opportunity while continuing to lose weight. Veterinary help must be obtained if a condition of this type is suspected. Otherwise, try to prevent a dog scavenging by placing food out of reach, and keep a close watch when you are out walking in case the dog finds the discarded remains of a picnic such as a chicken carcass. It is always possible that digestive troubles such as vomiting or diarrhea or a combination of these symptoms will follow scavenging.

MY DOG INSISTS ON EATING GRASS. IS HE LACKING ANYTHING IN HIS DIET?

Probably not, but you could try increasing the level of fiber, especially if the dog is prone to constipation. Eating grass seems to be natural behavior; it is often followed by vomiting which presumably relieves some irritation. Puppies may vomit roundworms by this means. Check that your dog is not eating grass that has been treated with chemical sprays. Most dogs prefer thickish stems to ordinary lawn grass so this behavior is more likely to occur when you are walking close to an area of long grass.

A few dogs develop abnormal appetites for other more harmful things. If you take your dog to the beach, make sure as far as possible that it does not attempt to swallow pebbles. While the canine digestive tract is fairly tolerant of foreign bodies, pebbles can become stuck, causing more serious consequences.

I BELIEVE THAT MY DOG HAS A FOOD ALLERGY. IS THIS LIKELY?

Such problems are not unknown, but relatively little study has been carried out in this area. Now that a link between hyperexcitability in children and certain ingredients in prepared foodstuffs has been found, similar links in dogs may be found in the future. It is important not to confuse an allergy with the virtually immediate reaction to eating indigestible food. In the case of a dog that cannot digest the lactose in milk, for example, the resulting diarrhea does not come from an allergy to lactose, but from the inability of the body to digest it. Skin rashes often result from an allergy. A wide range of foods may be implicated, and it can be a time-consuming task to track down the most likely cause. Various items have to be removed from the diet in a strict sequence, to see when the irritation disappears. An immediate improvement is unlikely to be apparent. It will probably take several days.

? HOW HARMFUL IS OBESITY IN A DOG?

It has been suggested that no less than about 30 percent of the dogs in the United States are obese, and this figure is mirrored in other countries such as the United Kingdom. Certain breeds are more likely to become overweight than others — Beagles and Labrador Retrievers are especially susceptible. But the problem also affects small breeds such as the Dachshund. In this latter instance, obesity may well lead to intervertebral disk problems, to which Beagles can also be prone. Obesity more often affects bitches than male dogs, and neutered dogs are most at risk from becoming overweight. Obesity often becomes a problem in middle-age when a dog's level of activity declines.

? HOW SHOULD I REDUCE MY DOG'S WEIGHT?

First decide on the correct weight for your dog. If it is not a pedigreed animal, aim to reduce its weight to the level where its ribs can be clearly felt but not seen beneath the skin as a rough guide. Special obesity diets can be obtained from your veterinarian and should help to lower your dog's weight. Otherwise reduce the overall amount of food offered by about 40 percent. Keep a check on the dog's weight on a weekly basis. Weight loss in the smaller breeds should work out to about a quarter of a pound weekly and will be about treble this figure in the case of big dogs.

The majority of obese dogs are overweight because they are being given too much food by their owners. It is vital to cut out all snacks while the dog is on its diet, and to make sure that no food is being scavenged from neighbors during this period. Studies suggest that dogs fed on home-prepared rations are most likely to become overweight. The dog is receiving surplus carbohydrate which is not being used on energy expenditure and is thus converted to fat. On a diet, part of the body's fat reserves are burned to meet the energy demands and are thus gradually reduced with a corresponding loss of weight.

Once you have succeeded in slimming your dog down to a better weight, try to insure that it does not become fat again. Increase the amount of food offered by about 20 percent so it is receiving just 80 percent of its previous food intake. Obesity does not always result from excessive feeding, but hormonal changes with a similar effect are quite rare in dogs. In severe cases of obesity, a veterinarian may recommend hospitalization so the dog can be placed on a crash diet with only water being provided.

Obesity is more likely to affect middle-aged dogs and the risk of obesity increases with age, as the level of activity declines and food intake remains constant. The side effects are especially noticeable in warm weather, with the dog panting excessively, like this Labrador Retriever (*left*) — a breed that is particularly prone to becoming overweight when kept in a domestic environment. Interestingly, studies have shown that the majority of obese dogs also have overweight owners.

The water intake of dogs varies according to their diet and the prevailing environmental conditions (*left*). Excessive thirst however, can be indicative of certain diseases and is often linked with urinary incontinence.

Dogs enjoy drinking water from alternative sources to their feeding bowls (*right*). They also have a tendency to roll around in mud as soon as possible after a bath, to restore their body scent.

? HOW MUCH WATER SHOULD MY DOG DRINK? AT TIMES, IT DRINKS MORE THAN USUAL.

Always make sure that your dog has a clean bowl of drinking water available; change the contents every day. There is no fixed amount that a dog will drink during a day. The quantity consumed will vary, depending on such factors as its diet, the temperature and the amount of exercise it receives. Typically, dogs fed on a dry diet will drink more to compensate for the relatively low amount of fluid in their food. And in hot weather and following exercise, the dog's thirst will be increased. You may not even know how much the dog is actually drinking since water bowls alone are not a reliable indicator. Unfortunately dogs will often drink from other sources such as puddles, when out for a walk, and toilet bowls at home. The latter is particularly dangerous, especially if there are chemicals such as bleach in the water. Keep the bathroom door closed and the lid of the toilet down at all times.

Measure the amount of fluid that your dog is drinking by filling the bowl with a fixed quantity and noting how much is left at the same time the following day. There are various medical problems which may encourage a dog to drink more than usual. If you are concerned, see your veterinarian. As a guide, a dog about the weight of a Cocker Spaniel should consume an average of one pint when kept on a canned diet. Never withhold water from your dog even if it is incontinent. This could be fatal because the dog needs to make up the excessive water loss from its body. The only circumstance in which it may be best to prevent your dog drinking water freely is when it is vomiting, as drinking water can precipitate further vomiting and further loss of vital body salts. Provide only a small quantity after vomiting appears to have ceased and seek veterinary advice. Conversely, there may be occasions when you need to encourage your dog to drink. This is usually when it has an infection of the urinary tract, or has deposits such as bladder stones in the tract.

Your dog's water intake may be reduced if you are providing milk for it to drink. Remember that milk is not essential and cannot be digested properly by all dogs. Some individuals get a taste for tea, but this is probably because of its milk content and any sugar that may be present. Do not encourage your dog to drink any form of alcohol; this is potentially harmful, and dogs, like humans, can become addicted to alcohol, with similar consequences. If you are going to the beach for the day in the summer, take a supply of fresh water and a bowl for your dog. Otherwise, in hot weather especially, a dog may resort to drinking sea water, and this can prove fatal in any quantity because of salt-poisoning.

helps to establish the beneficial vitamin-producing bacteria in their intestinal tracts.

If a dog is suffering from a malabsorption disease, part of the food will pass through the digestive tract unaltered, and re-emerge in the feces. These are attractive to the dogs because of the undigested foodstuff present in them. A condition of this type requires veterinary attention; the behavior can be corrected by appropriate therapy for the original problem.

Nevertheless, in many cases there is no clear-cut explanation for *coprophagia*. Always try to clear up the feces as soon as possible after they are expelled from the body so the dog has no opportunity to eat them. It is also possible to lace the stools with a foul-tasting substance such as curry powder. Other treatment involves the use of a drug called Cythioate, normally used to control fleas, which will taint the feces and cause them to taste bad when eaten. In bad cases, it may be necessary for apomorphine (which induces vomiting) to be administered as soon as possible after the dog eats its feces. Shortly afterwards, the adverse effects of the drug will become apparent, and the dog will feel ill for a couple of hours or so. It then comes to associate the feeling of nausea with eating its own feces and should then desist from this practice. Obviously such a drastic remedy must be discussed beforehand with your veterinarian.

Some dogs show no interest in their own excrement but are attracted to that of cattle and horses in particular. The dog may eat the feces or (perhaps worse from the owner's viewpoint) roll in them, with cow dung being especially favored. While the eating of such excrement is carried out for basically the same reasons as given previously, the deliberate soiling of the coat probably results from a totally different cause. Two schools of thought exist: one maintains that the scent from the herbivore's feces disguise the strong canine odor and helps hunting dogs conceal their presence from potential prey; the other believes the smell may act to reinforce the dog's body odor.

The latter explanation seems more feasible in practice since dogs that have recently been washed often have the maddening habit of seeking out the excrement of herbivores to roll in at the first opportunity when out on a walk. Since a bath removes the usual canine odor, the dog may be seeking to reinforce its social status because it has been deprived of its natural means of doing so. Nevertheless, another bath will be necessary and the dog's access to such sources of feces will have to be restricted as far as possible.

❓ I WAS HORRIFIED THAT MY FRIEND'S DOG EATS ITS OWN FECES. WHY IS THIS?

Such behavior, known as *coprophagia*, is quite common in various mammals including not only dogs but also chimpanzees! Various reasons have been suggested for such behavior in dogs. It could be that the dog is suffering from a digestive problem, notably a deficiency of certain B vitamins or vitamin K which are normally manufactured in the gut by bacteria. By consuming its feces, it obtains these essential elements which otherwise would be lost in large quantities from the body. It may be worth supplementing these vitamins to see if this overcomes the problem. Yet such behavior appears to be addictive and is often seen in dogs that have been kenneled under fairly unsanitary conditions for part of their life. A bitch will frequently eat the stools of her puppies, and they may consume hers early in life. It may be that this

GENERAL HYGIENE

Regular grooming is recommended to remove dead hair from a dog's coat, and to spot signs of external parasites. Your dog will need to be washed periodically.

? **HOW SHOULD I WASH MY DOG?**
It is best to perform this task out of doors, particularly during the summer months, because it tends to be a messy procedure. Wear a protective plastic apron or some other waterproof clothing for the purpose. A suitable tub of metal or plastic should be half-filled with tepid water. Remember that a dog's claws are sharp and can puncture inflatable pools and scratch the enamel on a bathtub. If a dog is dirty, as after a walk in the rain, the only cleaning necessary is to stand it in a plastic tub or your bathtub or sink and rinse its legs and belly off with lukewarm water (without soap). What is important is to rub it down with a towel or use a hair-drier until it is dry.

For a general washing, use a mild baby shampoo or a suitable canine shampoo available from your pet store. There are various types available. Some are useful under special circumstances — to emphasize the coat color of a poodle, for example. If your dog is very dirty, with oil on its coat, for example, use one of the special detergent gels produced for this purpose. Otherwise avoid detergents, dishwashing compounds, and medicated soaps as these are likely to have an adverse reaction on the skin.

A dog that is used to being bathed from an early age will not resent the process nearly as much as one that has never been near the tub. First place the dog gently in the water, and then, with a clean bottle or pitcher, pour the water over him carefully, starting at the hindquarters and progressing forwards. Apply the shampoo as directed and work it into a lather. The head should be washed last, taking particular care not to let any shampoo run

WASHING YOUR DOG

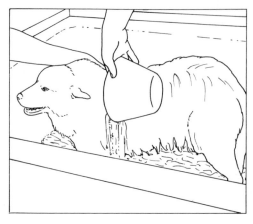

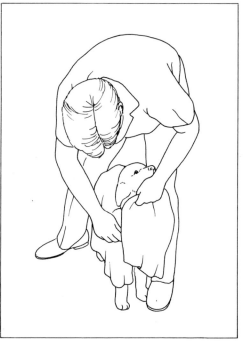

Outdoors is the best place to wash your dog. For hygienic reasons, it is preferable not to use the bathtub — although to new dog owners, it may seem the obvious place. Begin at the hindquarters and gently massage your dog. Insure all the shampoo is thoroughly rinsed and then dry the dog with an old towel. Dogs tend to shake themselves vigorously as well to remove most of the excess water. Wearing a protective overall is recommended.

into the eyes. By this time the dog is likely to have shaken itself, spraying water everywhere. It can be lifted out of the bath, and the dirty water poured out. Before the process is repeated, rinse the shampoo thoroughly out of the coat. Indeed, a hose can be used cautiously for this purpose, out of doors. It is then a matter of drying the hair after your dog has shaken off most of the remaining water from its coat. An old clean towel can be used initially for drying, followed by a hair-drier of some type for the final stage. The dog may be frightened by this apparatus at first so try to introduce it gradually and run it at a low temperature from the outset so as not to burn the skin. A brush used in conjunction with the hair-drier will speed up the process by serving to separate the hairs.

? HOW OFTEN SHOULD I BATHE MY DOG?

If your dog's coat becomes soiled with the excrement of other animals, it will need to be washed immediately. But it may not be necessary to give a full bath. Mud on the coat can be allowed to dry and then brushed out. Excessive washing of the coat is not to be recommended, as it removes the natural waterproofing agents and tends to make the appearance of the fur rather dull. A bath every three months on average will prevent the typical pungent "doggy" odor from becoming overpowering. It may be necessary to wash your dog before an important show, however, to create a good appearance for the judge. The use of hair conditioner is recommended by some owners to settle the coat after washing. This is because the coat carries static electricity after repeated grooming, and the negative charges involved tend to repel the individual hairs. A conditioner should help to neutralize them.

GROOMING ROUTINE

Besides keeping your dog's coat clean and healthy looking, brushing and combing can give mutual pleasure and so cement the emotional bond between the dog and owner.

? HOW SHOULD I GO ABOUT GROOMING MY DOG?

If you have a young puppy, get it used to the sensations of the comb and brush. More serious grooming can begin later, and the dog will then not be frightened of the procedure. The long-coated breeds need grooming on a daily basis. It is much better to spend a short time each day on grooming your dog than to neglect this task and then have to deal with mats. This will be painful for the dog, and it will come actively to resent the process. With a strange dog that seems not to like being groomed, place a temporary muzzle on it for safety's sake. If your dog has a heavily matted coat, take it to a veterinarian. He or she will be able to give a sedative and save the dog any further distress while the matted areas of the coat are removed.

In addition to improving the appearance of your dog, grooming provides a valuable means of detecting fleas and other parasites which may be present on the skin. Sharp burrs that could have become entangled in the coat while the dog was walking through undergrowth can be removed before they cause physical injury, and any superficial growths can be detected at an early stage. Dogs generally appear to find grooming pleasant once they are used to the process. And grooming helps to massage the skin.

When grooming, start at the head and run the brush or comb down the body in the direction of the fur. It is important that the dog stands on a firm surface at a comfortable height for the groomer. For the larger breeds, the task will probably have to be carried out with the dog on the floor. Smooth-coated breeds like the Beagle can be

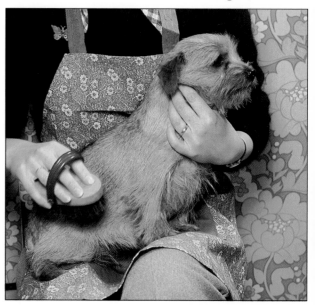

Red Setters (*left*) and other long-haired breeds are relatively more demanding as far as grooming is concerned and the job is easier if you stand your dog on an old table outdoors.

Grooming techniques do vary according to the breed concerned but for the smaller breeds it is easiest to sit the dog on your lap and use a dandy brush (*above*) to disentangle the matted fur.

54

GROOMING YOUR DOG

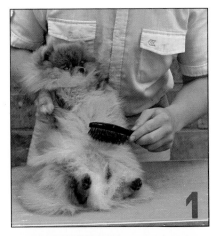

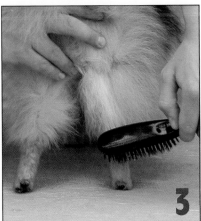

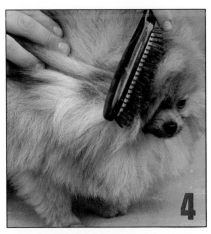

Begin with the stomach, using a brush and working with firm short strokes, brushing the hairs upwards, right from the roots (**1**). Also, try and loosen any tangled or dead hair.

To groom the rest of the body, start from your dog's back, working from the tail end, towards its head (**2**).

Then brush the "trousers" on both the fore- and hindlimbs, holding the tail to one side while you brush each hind leg down, gently but firmly (**3**). After the legs, brush the tail thoroughly, working from the root to the tip.

The neck and ears should also be brushed, carefully holding each ear while grooming the area beneath it and teasing out any tangles on the ears with your fingers (**4**), keeping the brush away from your dog's face. Lastly, groom beneath the head and under the chin, while holding your dog's head up with your other hand.

Using a comb rather than a brush repeat the procedure to remove any other remaining tangles (**5**).

The well-groomed Pomeranian (**6**) is displayed showing its soft bushy undercoat, long straight topcoat and abundant fluffed-up fur around the neck.

GROOMING THE HEAD

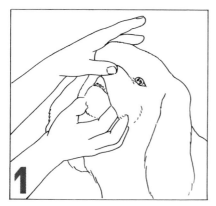

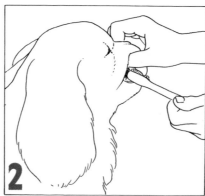

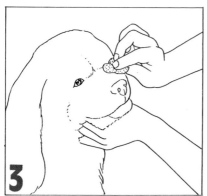

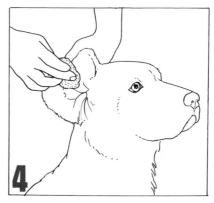

To open the mouth of an obstinate dog hold the lower jaw firmly with one hand and at the same time block the nostrils; inspect the teeth with special attention to the molars (**1**).

Using a toothbrush may hurt the dog's gums if they are sensitive and so it is preferable to use a damp cotton ball to remove superficial debris. Special dog tooth pastes are available (**2**).

Any tear staining, loose hairs or eyelashes can be cleaned away gently using a moistened cotton ball; use a fresh one for each eye (**3**).

The ears should also be groomed thoroughly and inspected for any signs of infection (**4**). Dogs with long heavy ears that hang down such as Spaniels, are most at risk.

Inspecting and cleaning a dog's teeth, usually by wiping them, should be routine (*right*) but, as many dogs are reluctant to open their mouths, it is important to encourage puppies to do this, from an early age.

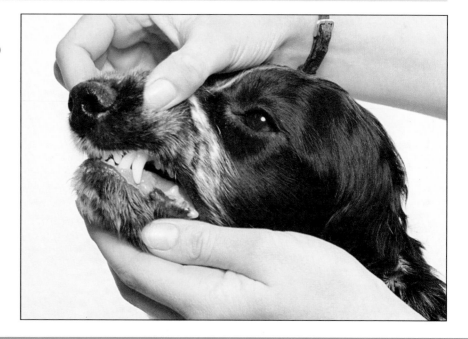

groomed with a hand glove. Dogs lose some of their hair throughout the year, but in the spring, the thicker winter coat will be shed. Another heavy shed will occur during the following autumn. At these times of year, grooming will take longer but it will prevent dead hair from being deposited around the home. A comb can be used on the finer points such as the so-called feathering, most noticeable at the back of the legs of breeds such as the Irish Setter. A comb avoids the need to brush around the eyes and other sensitive parts of the body. An overall grooming with a comb after a thorough brushing will remove any surplus dead hair and will insure there are no remaining clumps.

? **WHAT IS DRY SHAMPOOING? DOES THIS MEAN THAT I DO NOT HAVE TO BATHE MY DOG IN THE WINTER?**

Unfortunately, dry shampooing is no real substitute for a thorough bath. It is used mainly in show circles, and is not of great value. A powder, whose constituents remove surplus grease and dirt from the coat, is applied over the body and rubbed in well. A short time later, the shampoo is brushed out. The white color of the powder tends to make it unsuitable for use on dark-colored dogs, and it may cause the dog to sneeze, particularly when applied close to the head. A great deal of brushing may be required to remove all traces of the powder from the coat, and this in itself can generate a charge of static electricity which makes it difficult to settle the hair down properly. Never use a brush with nylon bristles as it will make this problem worse. Dry shampooing, therefore, has only limited applications and certainly will not remove heavy dirt from the coat. It may help to improve the appearance of dogs with pale coats without having to wet them thoroughly.

LOOKING AFTER THE PAWS

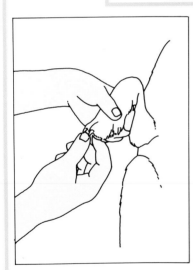 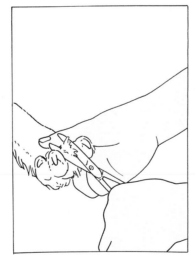 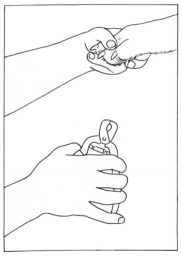

The space between the toes should be examined carefully for grit and small stones. If there is a grass seed in the dog's foot, it can be removed using a pair of tweezers but it is probably preferable to seek veterinary advice. Inspect the undersides of the foot pad in the same way and remove any embedded mud with a moist cotton ball.

Excess fur between the toes can be carefully trimmed away with round-tipped scissors, so as to minimize the risk of any infection.

Overgrown nails should be clipped with a stout pair of clippers, specially designed for the purpose. It is safest to simply trim off the sharpest points — never cut too short or near the quick.

POODLE PARLORS

The help and experience of professional groomers are likely to be essential for those who wish to show their dogs. Groomers also assist with other tasks, such as general clipping.

? WILL A PROFESSIONAL GROOMER WASH MY DOG? WHAT IS ACTUALLY INVOLVED IN THEIR WORK?

It is often part of the groomer's work to wash dogs brought to them. Certain breeds with long, silky coats may develop mats, and in severe cases, these will have to be cut away. Prior to bathing, the groomer will concentrate on removing the mats and combing the hair. Never bathe a dog with mats in its coat as these will then be even harder to extract, and the process will be more painful for the dog.

A large proportion of the breeds taken to grooming parlors are those whose hair needs to be clipped properly. This procedure is also carried out prior to washing, if required. The frequency of clipping varies somewhat according to the breed concerned. Poodles, for example, need clipping quite often — at least every two months, as do other dogs that do not shed their hair. Various types of clip are recognized with the so-called "lamb" clip finding favor with many poodle owners. The coat is trimmed to a uniform length, either short or long. The "Dutch" clip is slightly more ornate with short body hair contrasting with longer hair on the legs. The most elaborate clip, known as the "lion" clip, is usually seen only on show dogs since it is time-consuming and expensive.

Other breeds may also be clipped, depending upon the time of year. Old English Sheepdogs with their thick coats may well have their coats cut short during the warmer months. Spaniels also are clipped — usually about every two or three months. This provides an opportunity to remove some of the hair on the ears and helps to reduce the

Tidying and neatening up the shaggy and profuse coats of Old English Sheepdogs prior to a dog show (*right*) is in fact part of the general daily routine and care of this breed. Their coats are left shaggy for show purposes but sometimes, clipping of their coats is advisable, especially in warm climates. This can be done at home but most owners take their dogs to a professional grooming parlor for this purpose. Here, apart from being groomed, the dog may also be bathed and have its nails cut back, if they are overgrown.

Poodles as a breed are available in three sizes, from standard (*left*) to miniature and toy forms. Since they do not shed hair, they are frequently clipped in order to prevent matting of their coats, and this has become an accepted part of keeping many dogs besides show poodles, with regular visits to a grooming parlor being required every two months or so.

Styles of clip vary (*below*). The Lion or English Saddle style is favored by the British Kennel Club whereas the American Kennel Club does not discriminate between the Puppy, English Saddle or Continental styles. Poodle parlors will be able to advise on this aspect of show preparation.

Puppy

Continental

Lion or English Saddle

likelihood of the ear infections to which these dogs are prone. It is also not unusual to remove hair from between the toes. This is where the so-called eccrine sweat glands are, and the fur can become a source of irritation as well as a hiding place for harvest mites which have a similar effect. Clipping may also be required for medical reasons such as diarrhea, which would otherwise soil the coat around the anus and attract flies to lay their eggs among the matted fur, giving rise to the condition known as fly-strike.

The majority of wire-coated terriers will need to be stripped twice a year. This can be painstakingly carried out by hand using a tool known as a stripping knife. But even when undertaken by an expert, it is a slow and costly process. As a result, the showing of such breeds as the Airedale Terrier requires considerable dedication — for exhibition purposes, there is no acceptable alternative to hand-stripping. Most pet terriers, including the smaller Scottish and West Highland White, are just clipped with surplus coat being removed by means of thinning scissors.

AT WHAT STAGE SHOULD I HAVE MY POODLE CLIPPED?

The clipping of a poodle can begin as early as 12 weeks of age. It is important to get them used to the sound and sensation produced by electric clippers while they are still young so they will not resent the process in later life. Young poodles are usually given the "puppy" trim at first. This is fairly basic and resembles the "lamb" trim. If you are interested in learning to clip your own dog, join one of the grooming courses that are organized in various regions. These are often advertised in dog magazines. In some countries clipping can prove a worthwhile career for someone who is keen to work with dogs but lives in an urban area where there are few opportunities for kennel workers.

THE TRAVELING DOG

At some point a dog will have to be transported by car and will probably adapt fairly well to this experience.

? **MY PUPPY HAS GROWN INTO QUITE A LARGE DOG. WHAT IS THE BEST WAY TO CARRY HIM NOW?**

Probably by grasping it with your right arm around the back of the hind legs and your left arm extending under the neck. Smaller dogs may be supported under the chest. If you ever have to handle a nervous dog though, it is probably safer to dispense with the arm around the hindquarters and support this area with your elbow using your arm to grasp behind the forelegs. Your other hand can hold the dog's scruff so that it is unable to turn round and bite you.

? **IS THERE ANYTHING I CAN DO TO OVERCOME THE PROBLEM OF MY PUPPY BEING CAR SICK?**

Actually it is best to take your puppy out in the car several times, not just to the veterinarian's, in the early weeks. In this way, he will become accustomed to traveling by this means and should not associate it with a probably distressing visit to the veterinarian's office. Perhaps surprisingly, it is usually young adult dogs rather than puppies that suffer from car sickness. A conflict arises between the senses of vision and balance, and this triggers the vomiting response. In order to minimize the effects, do not feed your dog for four hours or so before you travel. Be sure that ventilation within the car is good, and do not get angry at the dog if it vomits. This is a reaction over which it has no control. Try to avoid long journeys at first, and stick to local trips. In this way, the dog will get used to the car, and the risk of car sickness is reduced. Be careful if your dog likes to stick his head out of the

CARRYING A DOG

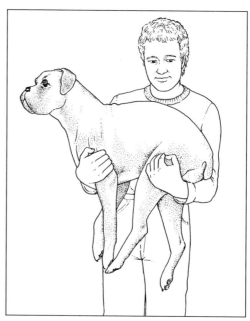

Whenever a dog is carried, it must be well supported — small dogs present fewer problems than their bigger counterparts. The chest provides a convenient means of support; never lift a small dog simply by its neck, leaving the remainder of the body dangling.

Dog guards (*left*) alleviate the possibility of traveling dogs distracting or impairing the visibility of the driver. Try to accustom and familiarize your dog to traveling from an early age.

window while the car is moving. This can be dangerous as he may get something in his eye or even try to jump out.

? MY DOG WILL NOT BEHAVE IN THE CAR. CAN I GIVE HIM A SEDATIVE?

Just as a veterinarian may prescribe treatment for chronic car sickness, so may he give a sedative to control a badly behaved dog in a car, but this is really only a last resort. Many dogs look forward to going out in a car and get into a state of great excitement because it means they will be having a walk. If your dog persists in leaping about and barking while in the car, tell him firmly to be quiet. Then park the car and disappear from sight for a few moments. Ignore your dog at this stage — if you make a fuss over him, he will think that you want to encourage this behavior. The delay in reaching the site for the walk means that the dog will not have achieved his aim. It is important for the dog to realize that not every trip in the car will end in a walk and run, particularly if the owner travels a lot with the dog.

A word of caution about leaving dogs in cars. The heat in the interior of a car builds up frighteningly fast. Never leave your dog alone in a car with the windows closed, especially during the summer months. In an emergency, try to park in a covered or underground parking lot, out of the direct rays of the sun. It is no exaggeration to say that dogs can die within minutes from the effects of heatstroke.

Like babies, dogs prefer to be held firmly and securely, in close contact with their owners and with plenty of body support (*above*).

THE SOCIABLE DOG

Firm leash training and plenty of exercise help to produce a happy, responsive and obedient dog.

?

SHOULD I USE A CHOKE CHAIN FOR TRAINING MY PUPPY?

The choke or check chain is certainly useful for training purposes providing that it is of the correct size and is worn properly. Make sure that you state the size of your dog to the sales clerk when you purchase the choke chain. As an approximate guide, the length of the chain should be equivalent to the circumference of the dog's head, measured across the ears and down under the throat, with an additional allowance of 2 inches. The individual links in the chain should be as broad as possible, so as not to tighten excessively around the neck.

If the choke chain fits correctly the free ring will slide beneath the throat rather than above it once the chain is connected to the lead. In this position,

the chain will not remain tight around the neck unless the lead is pulled. If you are in doubt, loop the chain around the dog's neck, so the rings meet by the left ear. The uppermost ring, running over the dog's head, is the one that should be attached to the end of the lead. It is vital to insure that the chain is fitted correctly; otherwise, the chain will be uncomfortable for the dog and may actually cause injury. This may be bruising or more serious nerve damage.

The main purpose of a choke chain is to keep a dog from pulling ahead of its owner. As it attempts to do so, the chain tightens, causing discomfort, so the dog learns to pace itself, avoiding the unpleasant sensation of the chain. If you decide to use a choke chain for training purposes, start by encouraging your dog to heel. Do not allow the dog to have too much loose lead (especially if you use a nylon retractable type) and begin walking with the dog on your left side. A young dog unused to walking on a lead is likely to start pulling ahead. Do not stop but continue at your pace. Jerk the lead once to tighten the choke chain, and give the command "heel." Your dog will soon come to realize what is expected of him. As always, give him every encouragement when he responds correctly. Once actually out on the street, your dog may start falling behind, having been attracted by a scent. Repeat the process, as if the dog was pulling in front of you, and give the same command.

It is particularly important to have a dog behave properly in towns. Always make your dog sit when you are waiting to cross a busy road. Otherwise, it is quite possible for an untrained dog to get hit by a passing vehicle if the dog should step unexpectedly

FITTING A CHECK CHAIN

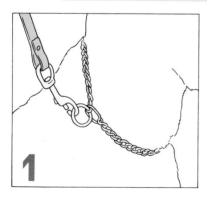

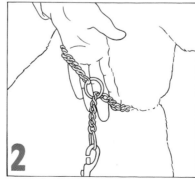

A choke or check chain must be fitted properly to insure it. In the correct position (**1**) the chain will automatically loosen when pressure is relaxed, whereas, if it is back-to-front, the dog will be harmed (**2**). Remember that the dog's everyday collar must be removed before a choke chain is worn.

1

2

The use of choke chains is not favored by everyone because the sensation that the dog experiences may be unpleasant and so deter the dog's enthusiasm for walking on a leash. Dogs' collars should always be adjustable and properly fitted — not too tight and not too loose — like the choke chain on this French Bulldog (*left*), insuring that the dog cannot be caught up by its collar.

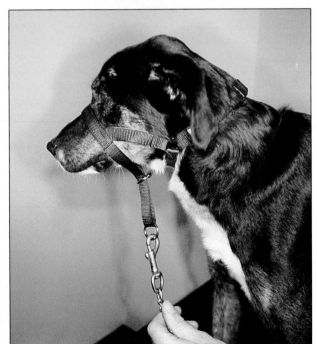

The Halti (*above*) offers a new approach to controlling a dog while it is being taken for a walk on a leash. The straps, reminiscent of a horse's nose band, fit snugly round the dog's face restricting movement of the head, and thus controlling the body.

into the road. The start of this training procedure again should begin in a yard or park. For increased realism, try to pick a spot where there is a path which can act as the road and grass representing the sidewalks on either side. As you approach the edge of the grass, give the command "sit" immediately before stopping. At the same time, tighten the lead slightly. This will tighten the choke chain and serve as an instruction to stop. At first, the dog will probably be reluctant to sit. Apply gentle pressure to the hindquarters as you did when you first taught your dog to sit prior to feeding it. As always, do not forget to praise him when he responds correctly.

If you feel that a choke chain is a piece of equipment you would prefer not to use, there is another option which has recently become available. Designed by a British animal behavior specialist, Dr Roger Mugford, the "Halti" works on the principle that if one has control of the dog's head, then control of the body is straightforward. Manufactured (mainly for the British market) in six sizes, the Halti is suitable for large and small dogs. It is rather reminiscent of a horse's nose band in appearance with a strap across the bridge of the nose which connects to a lead. There is said to be no risk of injury with this device.

? AT WHAT AGE SHOULD I START TRAINING MY DOG TO HEEL?

Certainly by the age of six months, young dogs should be expected to walk correctly on a lead. Do not be surprised if, on your first trip out, your dog fails to respond as you wish. The distractions of strange scents, other people and dogs, as well as the noise and bustle of traffic, will contribute to a loss of concentration. For this reason, it is useful to take your dog out as soon as possible after the vaccinations have been completed.

? HOW SHOULD I GO ABOUT LETTING MY DOG OFF THE LEASH FOR THE FIRST TIME?

Sound basic training should precede this stage. It is particularly important that your dog stays when told to do so. The extendible leashes are very valuable for teaching this procedure, but a standard leash can also be used for this purpose, once the young dog will sit, walk around in a circle giving the command "stay." At first, your dog is likely to follow you around, refusing to remain stationary. Break off, make it sit again, and repeat the process. With an extendible leash, you can move farther away from your dog, instructing it to stay and addressing it by name as always. Once this stage has been passed, it is a question of combining "stay" with the command "come." The leash can be gently pulled, if the young dog is reluctant to come forward when called. Give it ample praise when it responds as you wish.

These procedures should then be mastered with the dog free in the yard or a similar enclosed space where there will be no other distractions. When you first let your dog off the leash in an open area, choose a quiet spot well away from traffic and run through the commands with the dog on the leash first. Then you can walk away for a short distance before releasing your dog. Keep in constant touch with it, calling it back and rewarding it with a tidbit several times during the walk.

This will help to insure that you can catch it without difficulty when you want to put it back on the leash again. Hold it by the collar before offering the tidbit. Some young dogs delight at coming back to their owners but resent being caught. If your dog does run off, try not to run after it, but call it. After the initial surge of energy, it is likely to return. If you set off after it, it will assume this a game of some sort. However, some dogs are hard to leash train because of their natural inbred inclination to range all round an area as they pass by.

A well trained Lurcher (*right*) will rarely stray far from its owner when off the leash, although scent hounds such as Beagles may well pursue a trail, ignoring the owner's wishes. However, dogs should always be closely supervised when off the leash, particularly when in the vicinity of livestock.

A familiar, enclosed space such as your backyard is the perfect site for training your dog to obey your commands. His behavior in this environment is a good indication of his response to the delights and freedom of the great outdoor world awaiting him.

MY DOG CERTAINLY ENJOYS HIS WALKS — BUT HOW FAR SHOULD I TAKE HIM?

This will depend to some extent on the breed or size of the dog concerned. Regular periods of exercise are much better than long walks on weekends. These do little to promote fitness in your dog. Distance also depends on where you take your dog — if you can let him off the leash, he will clearly cover much more ground than you running back and forth. Young puppies should not be exercised excessively; this applies particularly to the giant breeds which develop slowly. Such dogs can suffer from muscular and joint disorders if they are taken on long hikes before they are mature. Up until the age of six months or so, your dog will probably not be sufficiently well-trained to be let off the leash when out for a walk.

The best guide as to whether your dog has had enough exercise is its response when you get home. If it soon settles down to sleep, then its walk will have been long enough. If the dog shows no sign of fatigue, then it is likely that additional exercise could be recommended. Small breeds probably will be content with a walk of up to one mile daily, but larger, mature dogs may cover at least ten times this distance. To save you walking so far, train your dog to retrieve a rubber ring. This will serve to reinforce the bond between you, and provide extra exercise and training for your dog. Retrieving is a natural instinct linked to hunting behavior. But remember that no dog should be allowed into a field where there are sheep or other farm animals when out on a walk. Even if the dog does not harm the sheep directly, it may cause panic and this could affect the health of pregnant ewes.

EXERCISE REQUIREMENTS

Chihuahua
Average daily walk: ½ mile

West Highland White Terrier
Average daily walk: 1 mile

Labrador Retriever
Average daily walk: 8 miles

Greyhound
Average daily walk: 3 miles

Irish Wolfhound
Average daily walk: 9 miles

Great Dane
Average daily walk: 6 miles

The length of walk that a dog requires varies considerably according to breed and other factors such as the dog's age and state of health. A "Westie" for example enjoys a good walk whereas a Chihuahua is more than happy with a short stroll each day. In all cases, regular walks are preferable, rather than marathon sessions at irregular intervals. Remember that the mileage required by each dog, according to this chart (*left*), does not mean that the owner has to walk this distance — a dog will run to and fro, covering at least twice as much ground.

 I'M THINKING OF PUTTING UP AN EXERCISE CHAIN IN MY YARD FOR THE DOG. ARE THERE ANY PRECAUTIONS THAT I SHOULD TAKE?

There are various types of exercise chain available. In some cases, the dog is attached to a long chain linked to a pole driven into the ground. Or, the chain can be connected to a suspended wire via a ring, enabling the dog to run back and forth along its length, and for some distance on either side. Neither system is entirely satisfactory, especially the chain on the ground, because the dog may get caught up around a tree, for example, and the weight of the chain may injure its neck. It is necessary to use a metal link of some kind because the dog may chew its way through rope and escape into the yard or further afield. Indeed, restricting a dog in this way is no substitute for exercise, and dogs may become neurotic, noisy and vicious if they are tethered for long periods. Never use a

running chain without making sure that the dog has water within easy reach and some protection from the elements, including the sun.

CAN I OBTAIN FURTHER ADVICE AND GUIDANCE WITH REGARD TO TRAINING MY DOG? ARE THERE PROFESSIONAL DOG TRAINERS?

In many areas there are dog training classes in the evenings, usually on a weekly basis. You may find them advertised in the local paper, or your veterinarian may have details available. Apart from training your dog effectively, such classes also provide an opportunity to meet people with shared interests, and they can be socially rewarding. There are often beginners' and more advanced classes for those who wish to progress possibly to actual obedience trials. To some extent, this will depend on the breed concerned. Perhaps not surprisingly, dogs that have evolved to work with farmstock such

Drying your dog with a towel (*left*) after a swim is a good idea, not only to remove excess water but also as a means of sharing the enjoyable experience of close physical contact.

Swimming is a useful form of exercise, but should only be encouraged in safe patches of water where wildlife, such as nesting ducks, will not be disturbed. Some breeds show special affinity to water and enjoy playing in it (*above*).

as the German Shepherd Dog and the Border Collie are most frequently seen in obedience competitions. In contrast, some breeds are harder to train; the Chow for example is rarely seen in such trials.

It may well be possible to find a professional dog handler who will train your dog. Bear in mind, however, the close bond between dog and trainer — although your dog may respond well to the trainer, it may not respond automatically to you. The ideal compromise is to attend training classes and discuss particular worries or problems with the person in charge of your group.

? SHOULD I LET MY DOG SWIM? HE SEEMS TO ENJOY THIS ACTIVITY?

Some breeds such as the Newfoundland tend to be more aquatic by nature than others. Newfoundlands have even evolved webbed feet for the purpose. There is no harm in your dog swimming, it provides a good source of exercise. It may even be therapeutic, but make sure there is no risk of your dog drowning either because of a strong current or because it is unable to get out of the water. Furthermore, the water should be clean with no obvious oil or other contaminants on the surface. After emerging from the water, the dog will shake itself to remove water from its coat. It will be useful to have a towel in the car if you are traveling by this means, so that you can dry off your dog before leaving for home.

? IS IT POSSIBLE TO GIVE MY DOG TOO MUCH EXERCISE?

Yes. Older dogs, particularly those suffering from heart or joint ailments, may be happy just pottering around the yard for periods each day with a short walk in the early evening. Never take older dogs out during the heat of the day, as their thermoregulatory system begins to deteriorate.

BODY LANGUAGE

Dogs use a combination of body postures, facial expressions, vocalizations and scent markings to communicate their feelings to their owners and other dogs.

The "play-bow" (*above*), when a dog bends forward on its front feet and then bounds off for a short distance before returning, is indicative of wanting to play.

 WHAT ARE THE VARIOUS SIGNS THAT DOGS USE TO COMMUNICATE WITH EACH OTHER AND THEIR OWNERS?

The ears have a very important role in communication and are not just for detecting sounds. The posture of the tail is significant, and the fur along the back may also be used to signal the dog's mood. When a dog greets its owner, for example, it usually wags its tail while its ears remain in their normal position. In a wary encounter with another dog, the tail is carried low and the ears are also lowered. One dog circles the other to pick up their respective scents. Direct eye contact is usually avoided because this is a gesture typically associated with a challenge and aggression. Dogs rarely bite without first signaling their intention to do so, usually by snarling and baring their teeth. A dominant individual in any encounter will stand with tail and ears erect and often raise the hackles along the back to emphasize an aggressive posture. Faced with this challenge, a subordinate dog will normally turn away and retreat, sometimes being pursued for a short distance by the other. By following a clearly delineated series of gestures, dogs negotiate a potentially harmful encounter without an actual fight occurring.

Stylized behavior is also seen in other contexts such as in inviting another dog to play. The instigator drops down on to its forelegs in the so-called "play bow," with its hind legs standing. The dog may then leap up and bound about, wag its tail and in some cases bark to give further encouragement. A similar invitation is extended to an owner when a dog is in a playful mood.

The tail is a significant indicator of a dog's mood, recognized by both owner and other dogs — the familiar wagging being a typically friendly gesture.

SENSE OF SMELL

In addition to body language of this type, smell also provides a potent means of communication, both directly and indirectly. Dogs have a much keener sense of smell than humans, and it is for this reason that dogs always sniff each other when meeting. They start at the head and then switch to the inguinal region between the hind legs. The significance of scent markers, known as *pheromones*, has been increasingly appreciated during recent years. These chemicals are present in the urine, and male dogs especially urinate very frequently when out for a walk to leave traces of their scent for other dogs passing on the same route. Male dogs urinate by lifting one of their hind legs; this enables them to direct urine to a particular spot such as a lamp post to which other dogs will also be attracted. This behavior is not seen in young male puppies, however, which squat like bitches when urinating. There may be a hormonal cause for this behavior since dogs only start to urinate by this means after puberty. The actual administration of the male hormone *testosterone*, however, does not appear to have a direct influence other than increasing the actual frequency of urination once the puppies are independent of their mothers.

Feces also may convey a characteristic scent to a dog, and wild dogs certainly use their excrement as territorial markers. The anal sacs or glands produce a secretion which under normal circumstances is transferred to the feces. A dog rubbing its rear end along the ground is more likely to be suffering from impacted anal glands than leaving a scent trail. The scratching on the ground sometimes seen after urination or defecation, usually on grass or a similar surface rather than concrete, may however be a deliberate means of leaving an auxiliary scent. Between the toes of its feet, the dog possesses sweat glands that could leave a scent and the characteristic scratch marks would serve to attract other dogs to the spot.

Aggressive encounters between dogs are rare, since the subordinate individual usually backs down, although both will make threatening gestures, including snarling (*above*), up to this point. A distinct hierarchy is apparent in these Eskimo dogs, reminiscent of the pack behavior of their wolf ancestors.

Sense of smell is vital to dogs and they recognize each other on the basis of scent, either directly (*left*), or from scent markers, notably urine. A male dog is not suffering from incontinence if he attempts to urinate at each lamp post while out for a walk — this simply serves as a territorial marker.

? DOES THE BARK OF DOGS VARY ACCORDING TO BREED?

Barking is another means of communication available to the dog. There are considerable differences in the frequency of barking between breeds. Some dogs such as Greyhounds rarely bark while others, like the Chihuahua, can be extremely noisy. The Basenji is often said not to bark at all, but in reality these dogs are capable of making a noise despite the reduction in the size of their larynx. Dogs will bark for a variety of reasons ranging from excitement to fear. The characteristic baying of hounds probably has a more specific function — it may serve to keep the members of a pack in contact with each other if they become split up. There is a clear aggressive warning in a growl, while whining usually indicates an attention-seeking mood on the part of an adult dog. This sound is rarely made in the company of other dogs, but puppies will use it to indicate that they are cold and distressed. The dog has an ability to hear sounds of a higher frequency than humans, and for this reason can detect the sound of dog whistles that are inaudible to the human ear.

? HOW IMPORTANT IS THE SENSE OF SIGHT TO A DOG?

It is of relatively little importance compared with the senses mentioned previously, and, indeed, the vision of a dog is not as good as that of a human in daylight. Their eyes are most responsive to moving objects, and their sight can be acute in this instance. It is said that dogs are capable of recognizing a fox over a mile away. They also have a broader field of vision than humans but a greatly reduced ability to distinguish between individual colors.

A potentially aggressive encounter between two Border Collies (*above*) usually ends without a serious fight. The subordinate dog, with tail down usually retreats.

A DOG'S FIELD OF VISION

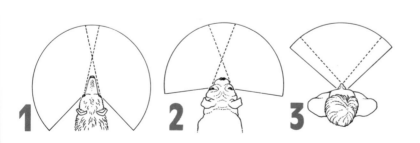

1   2   3

Dogs have a wide field of view because their eyes are located at the side of their heads. A dog with wide-set eyes can have as much as 270° (**1**), and a dog with more forward-pointing eyes normally covers some 200° (**2**) — still twice the angle achieved by the human physique (**3**).

The responsive look on this dog (*left*) gives some indication of dogs' superior sense of vision and hearing.
Their eyes are extremely sensitive to movement and their ears are tuned to frequencies well above the human ear. Also, dog's eyes are specialized — with a greater proportion of rod receptacles on the retina — to operate well in low light conditions.

A sign of subordination is displayed by the Boston Terrier (*above*), rolling on its back, while playing with a Dalmatian. This kind of behavior can also be seen in a domestic situation when a dog has been scolded.

? **THERE ARE A LARGE NUMBER OF DOGS IN THE AREA WHERE I LIVE. HOW SHOULD I ACT IF MY DOG IS ATTACKED?**

In most cases, the dogs will resolve the situation without direct conflict, but if you find that your dog becomes involved in a fight, try to walk on. Then call it. It will want to follow you and should make a rapid retreat. Contrary to popular opinion, there is little point in trying to separate two determined combatants. You may simply worsen the situation and get bitten yourself. If all else fails, throw a bucket of water over them, if you are in a position to do so. The main danger lies in the fact that an aggressive animal may refuse to acknowledge the effective signs of surrender. This applies particularly in the case of breeds kept originally for fighting purposes. When you are out with your dog, be sure that it remains in close contact with you. By this means, you should be able to prevent a fight before it starts. Male dogs are usually the worst offenders when it comes to fighting, and a few individuals will attack other males at every opportunity despite all attempts to train them to the contrary. If you have the misfortune to own a dog like this, make sure it is kept away from others. The only effective means of overcoming the problem is to have the dog castrated, because the aggression is likely to be of hormonal origin.

The **temperament** of German Shepherd Dogs — highly intelligent and slightly aggressive combined with acute scenting abilities — make them perfect for training as guard dogs (*right*).

Police dogs must learn behavior that human beings would find difficult and need specialized and patient training, the trainer having to assume the role of the pack leader (*below*).

? WHAT OTHER CAUSES ARE THERE OF AGGRESSION?

Obviously, a dog can become aggressive when protecting its own environment from strangers. This instinct is utilized in the training of guard dogs. The danger is always that an unsuspecting child may not appreciate a dog's warning signs. Similarly, a bitch with puppies will defend them if she feels they are threatened. Such aggression again stems from hormonal changes. This behavior may be unexpected, however, when the dog is suffering from a phantom pregnancy. Items such as toys are seen as substitute puppies, and even a straightforward attempt to take such a toy in order to play with the dog may be met with an unexpected and uncharacteristic display of aggression. Pain may also result in an aggressive response, and other medical problems, including brain tumors, can cause a dog to turn savage, as can the dreaded viral disease, rabies, in its "furious" form.

? HOW CAN I OVERCOME BEHAVIORAL PROBLEMS IN MY DOG?

This is a complex field of study and has been receiving increasing attention from animal psychologists in recent years. Many problems can be traced back to the owners themselves. A dog left on its own for long periods every day, for example, will get bored and in turn destructive. The remedy is obvious, but in practice it may not be possible to spend more time with the dog. Invariably the dog will either have to be moved to a new home or put to sleep. Indeed, major behavioral problems, ranging from aggression to soiling and destruction within the home, can often be traced back to poor training and a lack of interest on the part of the owner. In other instances, the dog may have achieved total dominance over its owner and the immediate family. Having bitten a member of the household, it may come to realize that it can retain this position by threatening to bite again. If you feel that you have a behavioral problem with your dog that you cannot overcome without help, refer first to your veterinarian. It may then be possible to consult an animal psychologist on recommendation from your veterinarian. You should probably find that you can claim a portion of the fees on your canine health insurance scheme if the veterinarian favors such treatment.

MY DOG DESTROYS MY HOME WHEN I GO OUT. HOW CAN I OVERCOME THE PROBLEM?

Once the permanent set of teeth have emerged (by seven months of age), the puppy's desire to chew is correspondingly reduced. It may be necessary to obtain a special spray in the interim to make furniture unpalatable to your dog. In an older individual, the destructive behavior may be a manifestation of the dog's worry about you leaving it or it could result from boredom or lack of exercise. It may also be a combination of these factors.

Try to accustom the dog to your absence for short periods, no longer than 10 minutes at a time, and give him a suitable chew toy before you leave. When you return and find the home undamaged, praise him. If he has reverted to his former habits, take no notice of him. Repeat the procedure at another time until the dog realizes what is expected of him and that you are not abandoning him when you leave him alone for short periods. Gradually, extend the time that you are away until he gradually becomes more used to his own company.

It may be that your dog also howls when you are out. Keep an ear open for such behavior as it can prove a source of valid complaints from near neighbors. While barking at the approach of strangers to the home can be beneficial, this activity should be controlled. Tell the dog to be quiet and praise it when it stops barking as requested. If it persists, it may need to be hit firmly but not hard to encourage him to desist. Electric-shock collars should not be used, even in countries where their sale is permitted, because the problem can be corrected by more humane means. Similarly, the cosmetic operation known as *ventriculocordectomy*, surgical muting of a dog, cannot be condoned.

Destructiveness is an inherent feature of many dogs' temperaments but, in the same way as children, they can easily be trained to play with a stick (*left*) or toy rather than devastating your home.

DOMESTIC MATTERS

Keeping a dog is not without drawbacks, especially at vacation time, although with advance planning, it should be possible to find a good local boarding kennel.

 MY DOG KEEPS ESCAPING FROM OUR LARGE FENCED YARD. WHY IS THIS?

It may be that the dog is attracted to a bitch in heat in the area. Some male dogs are chronic wanderers and escape at every opportunity. Check that your fences are as secure as possible; if your dog escapes and causes a road accident, you could be held liable for resulting damage. A companion may lead to a decrease in wandering. In male dogs, castration invariably has a noticeably beneficial effect on such behavior.

 IS IT WISE TO LEAVE MY DOG AT HOME WHEN I GO ON VACATION? MY FRIENDS HAVE OFFERED TO FEED HIM.

In spite of your friends' offer, it is probably best to arrange alternative accommodation for your dog while you are away. It is likely to pine in the home on its own for most of the day, and behavioral difficulties may develop. Your friends might agree to stay at your home or to have your dog at their home so it is not left almost totally alone for the whole day.

 IS IT A GOOD IDEA TO TAKE MY DOG ON VACATION WITH ME?

Various factors must be considered here. If you are going abroad, check to see whether you can take your dog with you; quarantine regulations may make this impossible. You should also consider whether your dog would fit into the kind of vacation you are planning. Some hotels will accept dogs (on payment of an additional fee), but you should check this as early as possible in case you have to make alternative arrangements. Remember, if your dog does come with you, it will be in a strange environment. It is vital that you can control it adequately so that it does not run off and disappear. When traveling by car, remember to take food and water bowls, a supply of clean drinking water, your dog's usual food (and a can-opener if necessary) and a familiar blanket to encourage it to settle down at night.

HOW CAN I FIND A GOOD KENNEL?

Probably the best means of finding a well-run kennel is to get a recommendation from friends. It can be very difficult to get your dog into such an establishment during peak vacation periods, however, unless this is organized well in advance. Satisfied customers return with their dogs year after year. Before deciding on a particular kennel, you may want to visit it. If so, arrange a convenient time. Any worthwhile kennel will be happy to have you to visit and discuss

Boarding kennels may appear rather formidable places (*left*), surrounded by wire fences, yet most dogs readily settle in to a well-run establishment.

arrangements. Notice how the dogs are housed. Is the place clean? One of the best indicators of the caliber of the staff is the way they respond to the dogs there. Small points such as referring to dogs by name indicate an interest in their work, and this is bound to be reflected in the care given to the animals concerned.

Check with them on inoculations. Most reputable kennels will want proof that your dog has received a current set of inoculations. Do not despair if you have lost or cannot find your certificate; your veterinarian may be prepared to issue a duplicate based on the records held at the office or confirm in response to a telephone call from the kennel that the inoculations were carried out on a particular date. This extra work may, of course, involve you in extra expenditure. The better kennels by and large tend to be more expensive. If your dog has a particular medical problem necessitating regular treatment, tell the kennel in advance in case it is unable to accommodate the dog with special needs at that particular time. In an emergency, your veterinarian may be prepared to hospitalize a patient who is receiving regular medication if the local kennels are unable or unwilling to assist.

Ask the kennel what, if anything, it would like you to provide when you take your dog in. Although many kennels look rather like prisons with wire to prevent escapes, the vast majority of dogs, unlike cats, settle very readily after a few days. Nevertheless, a favorite blanket or toy is likely to be appreciated and may assist in the settling-in phase. Generally, older dogs prove the least adaptable and may pine if they are not used to kennel life. If you are going away for any length of time, make sure that the kennel staff are aware if you have a bitch that may come into heat during this period. Again, some kennels will not take bitches at such times because of the disturbance they cause in the community as a whole. There are ways of preventing a heat (see p.83), providing that arrangements are made beforehand. If possible, leave your telephone number.

WOULD IT BE BETTER FOR MY DOG TO BE HOUSED IN AN OUTSIDE KENNEL?

No, not unless you intend to keep him solely for working purposes. A family pet that doubles as a guard dog should be integrated into the home as far as possible. You can provide an outdoor doghouse in the yard as a resting place for your dog. It is possible to purchase wooden doghouses from shed manufacturers; they are often on display at larger garden centers. Check that the wood has not been treated with any toxic chemicals in case your dog starts to chew the structure. If you want to paint the doghouse, avoid lead-based paints as these are poisonous.

Set the structure on a base of bricks and a damp-proof material such as a thick plastic sheet. The actual site chosen should be in a relatively sheltered and cool part of the yard. Wood provides a snug environment but has a limited lifespan. A more permanent structure can be built using cement blocks; these provide more insulation than bricks but may be subject to planning controls. If the interior is plastered, it will be easier to clean. Structures of this type are expensive, however, and clearly not portable.

WE ARE MOVING TO A NEW HOME, WITH MORE LAND THAN WE HAVE AT PRESENT. WILL OUR DOG SETTLE WITHOUT PROBLEMS?

The majority of dogs are not too perturbed by a move and soon settle in new quarters with the family. You will have to be sure though that any fencing is secure so that your dog will not be able to escape and start roaming the streets. There should be no problem over toilet-training at this stage, but some dogs may soil the home occasionally until they are used to the routine. In order to prevent this problem arising, repeat the early puppy training. Take your dog out to the selected spot in the yard and encourage it to "be clean," or whatever phrase was used previously. In this way, your dog will soon come to realize what is expected of him in the new environment.

I HAVE BEEN OFFERED A JOB ABROAD, AND WISH TO TAKE MY DOG WITH ME. HOW SHOULD I GO ABOUT THIS?

This could be a costly move, especially if you are just going for a short period of time. It may be preferable to see if you can find someone to look after your dog for you in your absence in view of

quarantine regulations. At present, for example, if you live in the United States and come home from abroad with your dog, you have to have your pet quarantined at a United States Department of Agriculture (USDA) animal center. Although the staff in such premises are dedicated, there are clear restraints on their involvement with individual dogs undergoing quarantine. You will be able to visit your dog during this period, but such separation can be very disturbing for a dog, especially if it is middle-aged and used to a close relationship with its owner. It is possible to find people who will take your dog while you are abroad for less than a standard kennel charges, and treat it as a member of their family.

If you do decide to take your dog with you, find

Outdoor kennels are not conducive to creating a close relationship between an owner and a dog. However, a dog will happily live in a kennel if it is warm, located in a sheltered spot, out of direct sunlight and within easy reach of fresh water (*left*).

Air freighting a dog around the world is relatively safe (*right*) but the various regulations should be investigated prior to the journey. There are companies that undertake the movement of your dog on your behalf.

Various designs of outdoor kennels are commercially available. Ideally, a wooden structure should be mounted on a brick base and only chemically safe preservatives used on the woodwork, in case the dog chews its quarters.

out from the relevant embassy what is required in the way of paperwork, tests and compulsory inoculations. Keep copies of all letters for future reference if necessary. Requirements can change from time to time. Before returning, contact the relevant government department — importation of dogs is usually under the jurisdiction of a country's agricultural ministry or equivalent body.

HOW DO I FIND OUT ABOUT SHIPPING MY DOG BY AIR?

You can contact one of the livestock shippers who are used to moving dogs by air, and ask for information. They will usually handle all documentation for you and arrange the necessary crate. Standards are laid down by the various airlines. A rabies vaccination (see p.123) is required for all travel abroad and is necessary for re-entry into the United States. An official health certificate should be no older than five days and sometimes has to be translated into the language of the country in question and notarized by the consulate. It is best to inquire about appropriate procedures well ahead of time at the local office of the USDA.

If you want to travel with your dog in the passenger compartment, check with the airline in advance to see if this will be possible. A suitable container will still be required, and the dog will be invoiced as accompanied baggage. Various governments do not permit the carriage of dogs in this manner on aircraft landing in their territories, and the dog will then travel as "invoiced cargo".

BREEDING

With probably millions of dogs being destroyed annually, simply because they are homeless, there is no justification for breeding dogs in a haphazard and irresponsible fashion, without planning. The factors and procedures are complex.

? AT WHAT AGE ARE DOGS SEXUALLY MATURE?

This varies. Some bitches show the characteristic signs of reproductive activity known as "heats" or "seasons" when only six months old, but most attain puberty by the age of a year old. Smaller bitches such as the toy breeds are likely to be reproductively mature earlier than their larger relatives although they are still growing at this stage. It is not usual to mate a bitch at her first heat.

In the case of male dogs, a similar pattern is noted with the majority being mature during the latter half of their first year of life. Males of certain breeds such as the Beagle may attain puberty before a bitch from the same litter, but generally, they mature slightly later than their female counterparts. This gap may extend over several months in the Chow. In any event, male dogs are not usually used for stud purposes until they are at least a year old. It appears that environmental temperature may have a bearing on the age of maturity, and socialization with other dogs tends to lead to earlier reproductive activity than isolation, as with a dog that lives on its own in a household.

? HOW DO I RECOGNIZE THE SIGNS OF HEAT IN MY BITCH?

You may notice that her vulva tends to enlarge. This is the first stage. It is known as the onset of heat (called *pro-estrus*) which lasts six to nine days. At this time she may be excessively playful. Male dogs will be attracted to her, but she is likely to rebuff any attempt at mating, possibly in an aggressive manner, even if she does not discourage their initial interest. Pro-estrus is signaled by a dark, bloody discharge from the vulva. Do not be surprised if your bitch urinates increasingly at this

MALE REPRODUCTIVE ORGANS

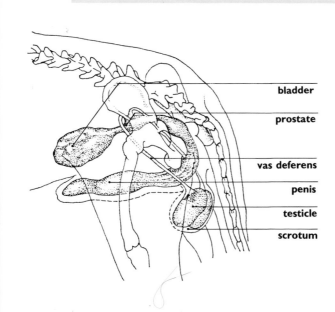

bladder

prostate

vas deferens

penis

testicle

scrotum

The testicles are situated in the scrotum and they vary greatly in size, according to breed. The spermatozoa and the male sex hormone testosterone are produced in the testicles, under the influence of the pituitary gland and various hormones. The distance of the the testicles from the body can be muscularly regulated, which also serves as a thermoregulatory mechanism. Males remain sexually active into old age, although their fertility declines.

stage. Such behavior is normal.

As the pro-estrus phase progresses, the bitch frequently licks this area, and spots of blood may appear on her bedding. Her appetite is likely to wane, and she may become more excitable.

At the start of the *estrus* part of the cycle, during which mating takes place, the vaginal discharge disappears. The estrus period can extend in length up to 21 days but usually lasts the same length of time as the pro-estrus phase. Therefore an average period of heat is considered to last about three weeks in total. Actual ovulation, the release of one or more eggs from the ovaries, normally occurs at the start of the estrus period, within 72 hours. The chemicals produced by the bitch, which serve to attract male dogs, gradually decline during the estrus phase, and then, if mating does not take place, the reproductive phase in the bitch's life is normally over until her next season.

The third phase, called *metestrus* begins when the bitch refuses to stand for the male. It lasts through the period of uterine repair — usually between 60 to 90 days. The fourth phase is called *anestrus*. It is relatively lengthy, and the vulva declines in size. After five months or so, the bitch will then enter the pro-estrus part of her reproductive cycle again, producing more *pheromones*, a scent that sexually attracts and arouses males.

Dogs readily detect a bitch in heat and will congregate around her (*above*), even if she is not in the receptive phase of her cycle — estrus. During the pro-estrus part of the cycle, the vulva swells and there is a bloody discharge from the vagina. This normally lasts about nine days.

FEMALE REPRODUCTIVE ORGANS

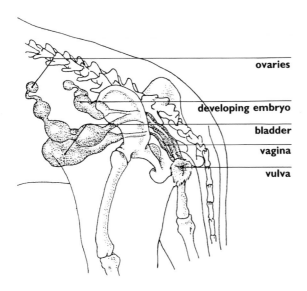

ovaries

developing embryo

bladder

vagina

vulva

The ovaries in the bitch are located in the dorsal part of the abdominal cavity, near to the kidneys, at about the third or fourth lumbar vertebra. The actual ovary is about half an inch long and the shape of a lima bean — its size increases during the pro-estrus phase, reaching its maximum at about the time of ovulation. The fallopian tube connects the ovary with the uterine horns which are long and elliptical and unite caudally, forming the uterine body.

SHOULD I LET MY BITCH HAVE A LITTER OF PUPPIES?

Allowing any bitch to have puppies requires careful consideration, so as not to add to the hundreds of thousands of dogs that have to be destroyed each year because they are unwanted. While it may seem attractive to have young puppies around the home, dogs grow rapidly, and the cost of caring for them rises accordingly. Indeed, breeding dogs on a small scale is unlikely to be profitable, especially if your time is taken into account. It may be possible to find homes for pedigreed puppies, especially if your bitch has been shown successfully, but mongrels will probably prove much harder to place with caring owners.

I INTEND TO BREED WITH MY PEDIGREED BITCH. WHAT IS THE BEST AGE FOR HER TO HAVE PUPPIES, AND HOW SHOULD I SELECT A SUITABLE STUD DOG?

Bitches are usually mated at their second heat or possibly the third in the case of larger breeds that mature more slowly. There is no point in rushing your bitch into having puppies since the demands of preganancy in addition to growth will not benefit either her or the resulting offspring in the long term. Although bitches will continue to have periods of heat throughout their lives and not undergo the equivalent of the human menopause, the reproductive success rate will decline from the age of about five years onwards. Most breeders therefore breed from bitches between one and five years old. Male dogs can be older, but their fertility also declines with age.

Choosing a suitable stud dog will require total honesty on your part. Look at your bitch with a critical eye and assess her faults as well as her strengths. You want a male dog that excells as far as possible where your bitch is weakest. Clearly, a study of pedigree will be important, and the guidance of an experienced breeder or judge can also be a great asset. If necessary, refer back to the breeder where you obtained your bitch. He or she will probably be pleased to help you and may later be interested in a puppy, especially if the bitch has done well for you in the show ring.

Arrange an appointment and then go to see the stud. Clearly, this should be undertaken early, so that plans can be made to mate your bitch at her next heat. Do not leave it until the end of the pro-estrus phase when it will probably be too late. The owner of the stud will be able to give you pedigree details and will probably want to be assured that your dog is fully inoculated. Discuss the stud fee, and ask what happens if mating is unsuccessful at the first heat. The breeder may offer a reduction if your bitch does not conceive, depending on the circumstances. Another area which needs to be discussed concerns the screening

Breeding dogs can be extremely rewarding and the finer, more subtle attributes of your pedigreed dog are especially appreciated at dog shows (*left*).

HEREDITARY DEFECTS

DISORDER	OBSERVATIONS	BREEDS TYPICALLY AFFECTED
Clefts of lip and palate	May be hereditary in origin, but other factors, such as a nutritional deficiency in the bitch, may also be responsible.	American Cocker Spaniel, Beagle, Bernese Mountain Dog, Boston Terrier, Bulldog, Dachshund, German Shepherd Dog, Shih Tzu
Deafness	Dog often appears unresponsive, even stupid, until this disorder is recognized.	American Foxhound, Bull Terrier, Collie, Dachshund, English Foxhound, Great Dane, Scottish Terrier.
Distichiasis	A double row of eyelashes most common on upper lids. Causes severe irritation and excessive tear production. Surgery is the only effective treatment in the long-term.	American Cocker Spaniel, Bedlington Terrier, Boston Terrier, Brussels Griffon, Kerry Blue Terrier, Lakeland Terrier, Yorkshire Terrier
Ectropion	Eyelids directed outwards. Causes inflammation of the conjunctiva and cornea, with increased tear production. Needs to be corrected by surgery.	American Cocker Spaniel, Bassett Hound, Bloodhound, Bulldog, Clumber Spaniel, St Bernard
Hip dysplasia	Deformed hip joints. Signs extremely variable: lameness in severe cases, yet may pass unnoticed in a mild case. Detected by radiography. Inherited, hence the need to check potential breeding stock for this weakness.	American Cocker Spaniel, English Setter, German Shepherd Dog, Giant Schnauzer, Shetland Sheepdog
Intervertebral disk abnormalities	Symptoms influenced by locality of abnormality, as is the prognosis for treatment. Total, confined rest is essential for recovery, irrespective of other therapy. Surgery can be of assistance in some cases.	American Cocker Spaniel, Beagle, Boxer, Dachshund, Dandie Dinmont Terrier, Pekingese
Luxating patella	Results in lameness, typically about five months of age. Caused by movement of "knee bone" or patella. Degree of weakness variable. Surgical correction is the only treatment.	Boston Terrier, Bichon Frise, Chihuahua, Pomeranian, Yorkshire Terrier
Progressive retinal atrophy (PRA)	The first sign may be that the dog appears to be having difficulty seeing at night. As its name suggests, this disease is progressive, and ultimately blindness will result. The time span may extend from months to years. It appears to be an inherited condition; different forms of PRA are believed to be inherited in different ways, so it can be either a dominant or recessive trait.	Border Collie, English Cocker Spaniel, English Springer Spaniel, Golden Retriever, Gordon Setter, Labrador Retriever, Pekingese, Pomeranian, Poodle, Samoyed, Shetland Sheepdog, Welsh Corgi
Umbilical hernia	Distinct, noticeable swelling around the umbilicus or "belly-button", resulting from a partial protrusion of the abdominal contents. Can be corrected by surgery if necessary.	Basenji, Bull Terrier, Collie, Pekingese, Pointer, Weimaraner

Responsible breeders will have their dogs checked for potential inherited defects, of which the most significant tend to be hip dysplasia and progressive retinal atrophy (PRA). There are a large number of inherited and congenital problems however, often linked with particular breeds.

of the stud dog for any inherited condition that may affect that particular breed such as *progressive retinal atrophy* (PRA). Be sure that your bitch is also checked by a veterinarian when applicable, as potential purchasers of the puppies are more enthusiastic if such evidence can be produced.

? HOW CAN I PREDICT WHEN MY BITCH'S NEXT HEAT WILL OCCUR?

On average, a bitch has two periods of heat each year, but in practice, this can be quite variable. Some people think that the smaller breeds have shorter intervals between heats than their larger relatives, but this is not necessarily true. German Shepherd Dogs for example have relatively short inter-heat periods, sometimes just five months, while Dachshunds can go for eight months between heats. The time lapse appears to extend from two months to as many as seventeen, and certain dogs may have irregular heats. This can make calculations difficult, particularly if you intend to mate the bitch on her second heat. Obviously the owner of the stud dog will be aware of this difficulty, so make a rough assessment when the heat will occur and notify him or her when you detect the start of the pro-estrus phase.

? DOES THE MALE DOG HAVE A PERIOD OF SEXUAL INACTIVITY LIKE THE BITCH?

No. Male dogs can mate throughout the year if there is a bitch in heat. When mating a maiden bitch for the first time, try to use an experienced male who knows what is expected of him. Conversely, a young stud dog is better placed with an older bitch who is less likely to resent him.

? **HOW IS THE MATING SUPERVISED? I HAVE BEEN ASKED TO LEAVE MY BITCH AT THE KENNEL WHERE THE STUD DOG IS HOUSED. IS THIS USUAL PRACTICE?**

It is normal for the bitch to be taken to the stud rather than vice-versa. The owner of the stud will make sure that your bitch is well cared for, and her stay there will insure that repeated matings can take place, thus maximizing the likelihood of a successful outcome to the liaison. If you prefer, you may want to take your bitch back and forth, but this could prove disconcerting for her.

Unfortunately, it is not possible to detect the time of ovulation in dogs by means of a slight temperature rise, as in humans. Vaginal smears studied under a microscope can be of some value, but breeders do not usually seek veterinary help of this kind. They are used to recognizing the characteristic signs of the onset of pro-estrus and can calculate the likely time of ovulation and the best day for mating. It is therefore vital that you determine as accurately as possible when pro-estrus began so that you can arrange for mating to commence approximately ten days later.

Much can be learned when the bitch is introduced to the dog. They will start sniffing each other around the genital areas. If the bitch is receptive, she will stand with her tail to one side, enabling the dog to mount her. Mating in the case of the dog is a lengthy process. Initially, the male rides on the female's hindquarters, gripping with his forelegs along her flanks. The tip of the penis swells with blood and erects fully in her vagina. At this stage, the so-called "tie" is formed — the bone known as the *os penis*, present in the male's organ helps maintain its position in the vagina for as long as three-quarters of an hour. A maiden bitch will probably show signs of concern and may attempt to break free. She will need to be carefully restrained from the front if she is not to injure her mate. Ejaculation follows with the semen emitted from the male's penis after secretions from the urethral glands which will help to nourish and protect the spermatozoa liberated into the female's reproductive tract.

Prior to the end of mating, the male will dismount and effectively swivel around so that the heads of the dogs are at their furthest points apart, while their bodies remain tied. At this point, further secretions from the prostate gland are liberated, and then the tie is dissolved. It is not necessary for a tie to occur in order for mating to be successful; indeed, Chows often do not form a tie when copulating. After one supervised mating, a second is usually carried out the next day and possibly a final liaison on the fourteenth day, following the onset of the pro-estrus phase to maximize the likelihood of reproductive success. Stud dogs should not be used excessively on the same day because their fertility will decline and they are likely to be tired after being locked with the bitch for an average of about 20 minutes.

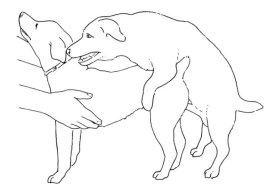

A tie is usually formed which lasts several minutes.

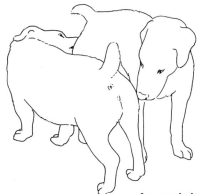

As a prelude, the dogs sniff each other's genital region and after a variable length of courting, the bitch will allow the male to mount, standing with her tail aside.

THE BULBOUS URETHRA

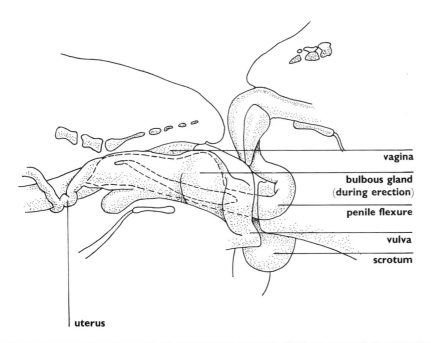

vagina

bulbous gland
(during erection)

penile flexure

vulva

scrotum

uterus

During intercourse, the bitch's vaginal muscle goes into spasm and contracts around the bulbous urethra — a gland that forms a hard, round, prominent swelling at the base of the penis. This gland plays an important part in holding the dog and bitch together. If the dogs appear stuck, the best course of action is to leave the animals alone.

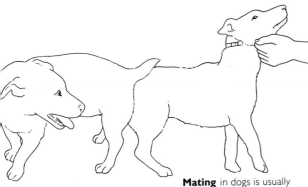

Mating in dogs is usually supervised, certainly at a stud. Some ailments can be transmitted by sexual contacts between dogs, notably the canine venereal tumor and Brucellosis. Any signs of abnormal swelling, possibly indicative of a tumor should be reported to a veterinarian without delay, and the dog should not be mated. Screening for Brucellosis is possible.

Finally, the dogs swivel round and remain standing quietly facing away from each other, joined in the genital lock.

? IS IT POSSIBLE TO PRODUCE PUPPIES BY ARTIFICIALLY INSEMINATING THE BITCH?

This method is quite feasible, providing it is carried out at the correct time. Indeed, there is a tendency for breeders to send semen for artificial insemination abroad. This is possible because fresh semen can be stored for a week without losing potency under the correct conditions and, once frozen, can be kept almost indefinitely. Nevertheless, there are health controls on the importation and exportation of canine semen because it can be a means of transmitting the rabies virus if the donor was infected. In addition, artificial insemination should be carried out with the approval of the governing body of the canine world in the country concerned if the offspring are ultimately to be registered. The technique is relatively straightforward. A pipette is used to introduce the semen into the bitch's reproductive tract with her hindquarters kept raised to prevent excessive loss of semen at this stage. Once the pipette has been withdrawn, a gloved finger is placed within the vulva orifice for five minutes or so. This mimics a brief tie and assists fertility.

PREGNANCY

It is virtually impossible to detect any visual signs of pregnancy in the bitch until the fourth week or so. The final part of the gestation period is the phase of rapid growth of the puppies. Phantom pregnancies are not unusual.

number of growing embryos. Each forms a placental attachment which provides vital nutrients as well as oxygen and removes the waste products of the embryo's metabolism. Since there is no direct connection in the placenta between the circulatory systems of the mother and her developing puppies, she cannot transfer immunity to them as occurs in the human. They will be dependent on suckling to obtain the vital protective immunoglobulins during the first days of life. By the 33rd day of pregnancy, the process of *organogenesis* has taken place, and for the remainder of the pregnancy the fetuses, which now resemble miniature puppies, grow to full term size. This is the major growth phase, the time when demands on the bitch are greatest during the pregnancy: 95 percent of the puppies' growth takes place in this stage.

WHAT HAPPENS IN THE BITCH'S BODY AFTER MATING HAS TAKEN PLACE?

The spermatozoa should fertilize the eggs that have been released from the ovaries to form *zygotes*, the beginnings of the embryos. These zygotes implant themselves in the wall of the uterus by about 19 days after mating. The embryos then start to develop. It is unusual for bitches to produce only one puppy. The horns of the uterus are quite long so there is adequate space for a relatively large

WHAT EXTERNAL EVIDENCE WILL THERE BE IF MATING WAS SUCCESSFUL?

In the early days, very little. But from the fifth week, the fetuses begin to grow in size and the abdomen of the bitch may start to appear distended. This will be most noticeable in bitches that are having their first litter. Simultaneously, their mammary glands will start to alter in appearance. The teats will swell in size and appear bright pink, reflecting the increase in blood flow to the region.

The final stages of pregnancy are most demanding for the bitch, as is apparent by this almost immobile, pregnant Basset Hound (*right*) — 95 per cent of the puppies' growth takes place during this period. This is so that the bitch is not forced to carry the puppies any longer than necessary when they are approaching their maximum weight.

EMBRYOLOGY

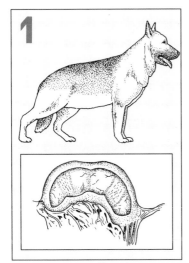

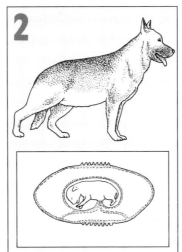

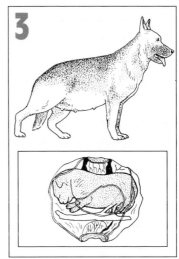

Signs of pregnancy will not be apparent until about the fifth week. After fertilization the egg becomes a zygote — a mass of dividing cells (**1**). The zygote implants into the uterine wall, and here the puppies develop, forming a placental connection with the mother.

The bitch becomes progressively heavier and by the fifth or sixth week her nipples and abdomen begin to swell. The embryo continues to develop, with the body organs being formed first. By the 35th day the head, and limbs are formed and the external sex organs can be differentiated (**2**).

As parturition approaches, the nipples become swollen and turgid, sometimes secreting milk and the abdominal swelling is typically pear-shaped. By the 55th day (**3**), fetal movements become visible in the flank of the bitch. The embryo is fully developed, complete with body hair, color markings and digital pads.

It may be possible for a veterinarian to confirm that a bitch is pregnant after a period of about 32 days by careful palpation. Some bitches refuse to cooperate however and tense their abdomens. In obese dogs or muscular dogs like Greyhounds, a clear indication may not be possible. At a later stage, it can be very difficult to distinguish puppies from abdominal contents. Ultra-sonic scans can be given by a veterinarian, and these can detect a pregnancy by the four-and-a-half-week stage. Never poke or prod the abdomen of your bitch to discover whether she is pregnant.

WHAT EXACTLY IS A PHANTOM PREGNANCY AND HOW DOES IT OCCUR?

A phantom, false or pseudo-pregnancy arises as a result of an ovarian disorder. Normally, after ovulation has occurred, structures known as *corpora lutea* develop at the sites where the eggs were released to replace the follicles that contained the developing eggs. These corpora lutea give off the hormone progesterone which ensures that the zygotes can implant themselves successfully into the walls of the uterus and stimulates the production of milk in the mammary glands.

In the case of pseudo-pregnancy, the corpora lutea continue to produce the hormone for up to three months. The bitch sometimes shows such typical signs of pregnancy such as swelling of the teats and actual milk production in some cases. This usually happens around the time that a litter would be expected if mating had taken place at the previous heat, but it may occur up to 10 weeks later. The temper of the bitch also changes. It may become fretful and often starts to seek out a suitable spot to nurture her phantom puppies. Toys often take on the role, and attempts to remove the toys are likely to be greeted with aggression.

Your veterinarian can prescribe pills to help her over this phase, but in the long term, spaying should be seriously considered. Breeding may worsen the problem over successive heats, and some people believe that persistent false pregnancies make a bitch more susceptible to an infection of the uterus called *pyometra*.

? HOW SHOULD I FEED MY BITCH DURING PREGNANCY?

There is no need to worry about dietary changes until the latter third of the pregnancy when the fetuses start to grow. At the age of six weeks, for example, the developing puppies in a Beagle bitch weighing 30 pounds are only about half an ounce each in weight. As a general guide, you should increase the amount of food offered by about 10 percent per week starting at six weeks after mating. It will also be necessary to divide the daily ration into several smaller meals because the growing fetuses in the uterus will restrict the stomach capacity at a time when the bitch needs a higher food intake.

? HOW SHOULD I EXERCISE MY BITCH DURING PREGNANCY?

In the early stages, carry on as normal, but in the latter part, your bitch may show a reluctance to cover her usual distance with you. Do not force the pace if she is reluctant to go far from home. By the end of the pregnancy she will be carrying as much as 15 pounds of additional weight, in the case of one of the larger breeds. She must be discouraged from jumping at this time, but some exercise is definitely to be recommended to keep her musculature healthy.

? WHAT SHOULD I DO TO PREPARE FOR THE BIRTH OF THE PUPPIES?

It is important to notify your veterinarian when you expect the litter to be born. As a general rule, the gestation period is approximately 63 days, but it can vary by as much as a week in either direction. If you have not had the bitch inoculated recently prior to mating, your veterinarian may recommend a booster using dead (killed) vaccines. Serious defects in the puppies are likely to result if living vaccine is given to their mother while they are still *in utero*. The booster will insure that the bitch has a high level of antibodies present in her milk when she starts suckling the puppies. Another important consideration is to deworm the bitch to reduce the infection being transferred to the puppies. Follow your veterinarian's instructions on this matter; larval worms present in the bitch will be triggered from their dormancy by the onset of pregnancy and can be spread to the puppies before they are born.

THE BIRTHPLACE

You will have to decide where the bitch will give birth in the home. A guest room is the ideal location, since here she can be kept quiet and warm with no unnecessary disturbance. If there is carpeting on the floor, cover this with a layer of

Encourage your bitch to use the whelping box before giving birth so that she readily accepts it. The box needs to be positioned in a quiet spot, such as a spare room, and lined with newspaper so that it can easily be cleaned. A simple cardboard box or even a quiet corner (*right*) may suffice in some cases.

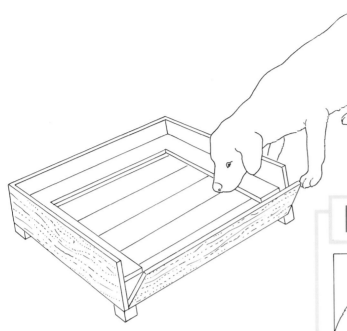

A **whelping box** (*left*), should include an anti-crush bar around the sides so that the puppies can escape from their dam, rather than being rolled on. The front should be hinged so that the puppies can either be let out, or kept in their box during the early weeks of their lives. The size of the box will depend upon the bitch herself. She will lie out flat to feed her litter, and needs to be able to do this without hindrance.

FEMALE GENITALIA

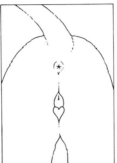
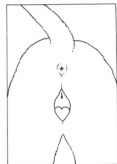

The vulva is normally dark pink and constricted (*above, left*). Just prior to whelping the vulva dilates and swells and changes significantly in color to a

bright, dark pink. The mammary glands may also swell.

plastic sheeting and place layers of newspaper on top. You will need a whelping box where the bitch can have her puppies. It does not need to be an elaborate structure. For the smaller breeds, a large cardboard box with the sides cut down and an easy entrance should suffice, providing that the quarters are not cramped. Remember the bitch will need to be able to stretch out to feed her puppies.

A wooden box, with sides about six inches high, can be easily constructed as an alternative. For the bigger breeds, an anti-crush bar around the internal surface is often recommended. This will prevent a puppy in a corner from being squashed or suffocated by the mother lying accidentally on top of it. A bar of this type should run horizontally about two inches down from the top of the sides, and extend out approximately three inches. One side can be hinged, so that the puppies can leave the box without difficulty when they are walking about. The interior of the whelping box should be lined with a layer of newspaper with an old towel or blanket on top. This will inevitably become soiled during the birth process and is then best disposed of. Encourage the bitch to sleep in the box, both during the day and at night.

WHAT ARE THE SIGNS OF BIRTH BEING IMMINENT?

It is important that the bitch feels secure with her whelping box. Otherwise she may choose to give birth in a less convenient location. She may even invade a bed for this period if she has an opportunity to do so. Early signs of birth being imminent are restlessness, loss of interest in food, and occasional vomiting. Constipation may also occur in the later stages and can be corrected by administering up to three teaspoonfuls of mineral oil, which can be obtained from a pharmacist. The most reliable indicator of birth is a fall in body temperature, from about 101.5 °F to 99.5 °F. The vulva also expands in size, and the two uppermost points of the pelvis above the legs appear more prominent, as the ligaments slacken in preparation for the birth.

THE BIRTH

The puppies will be born approximately 63 days after mating took place. The bitch should be encouraged to use a whelping box, located in a quiet part of the home where she can give birth to her litter undisturbed.

 HOW DOES THE BIRTH OCCUR?
In the first stage, the bitch will appear very uncomfortable and may start panting and shivering and be reluctant to settle. This can last for well over a day, but usually abdominal contractions heralding the second stage will be apparent within 12 hours. There is no need to stay with your bitch throughout this initial period. Simply offer her food and check her at regular intervals. About an hour into the second stage, the first puppy should emerge head first and still wrapped in the *allantoic* sac containing the fluid which protected it while it was in the uterus. After she has given birth to the first of her offspring, the bitch will break the covering, and lick the puppy vigorously to start it breathing. Within a quarter of an hour, the placenta which nourished the puppy through its early existence will also be expelled completing the so-called third stage of labor. While the puppies are being born, you should be on hand in case an emergency arises. Keep count of the number of placentas passed, to insure that it tallies with the number of puppies born. As a general rule, bitches will consume the placentas; this is normal behavior and not an indication of impending cannibalism towards the litter. The mother will normally bite the umbilical cord if the puppy retains its connection to the placenta. Puppies are usually born within half an hour of each other, but this time can extend up to twice as long without giving undue cause for concern, providing that the bitch does not appear distressed. The overall length of time for the litter to be born obviously depends on the number of puppies involved. The smaller breeds can have between one and six. Bigger dogs

BIRTH POSITIONS

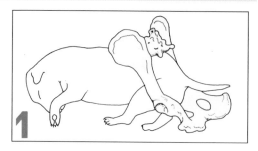

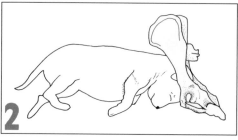

The position of the puppy immediately prior to birth may vary, and this can lead to complications. Under normal circumstances, puppies are born head first (**1**), but in a proportion of cases, they emerge tail first (**2**). This is described as a breech presentation, and may cause problems, although in most cases, this will rectify itself. It is a serious matter, however, if the puppy becomes twisted and stuck in the birth canal, and requires rapid veterinary attention.

may produce correspondingly large litters, up to 14 or so pups. In most instances, the birth process should be completed within six hours of the emergence of the first puppy, but with larger litters, the bitch may rest, prolonging the procedure.

WHAT PROBLEMS COULD I ENCOUNTER WHEN THE BITCH IS GIVING BIRTH?
The birth of puppies usually proceeds without difficulty but this varies somewhat according to the breed. In the case of dogs with broad heads such as the Bulldog, the puppies can get stuck in the birth canal, and may have to be born by Caesarian section. In addition, there is cause for concern when any bitch exceeds the anticipated time of delivery by more than a couple of days. The first condition is an emergency which requires veterinary assistance without delay. The second instance may not be critical. The point is that if you are worried at any stage, contact your veterinarian. There could be nothing worse than leaving the situation in the hope that it will sort itself out — this is often not the case.

If the bitch does not try to break open the membrane surrounding the puppy after birth, do so immediately at the puppy's head end by raising and pulling the covering apart. Wipe the puppy's face, paying particular attention to the nostrils and then rub it vigorously in a towel to stimulate its breathing. Placing a finger cautiously just inside the mouth and opening the jaws slightly, can have a similar effect. Should the puppy still be reluctant to breathe on its own, blow up its nostrils. With premature litters, it may be impossible to keep them breathing because they lack sufficient amounts of surfactant to inflate the lungs properly. If a veterinarian is on hand, he or she may be able to administer a suitable respiratory stimulant, but even this is no guarantee that such puppies will live.

If the umbilical cord is left intact by the bitch, break it, using clean hands. It is not as vital as breaking the membrane surrounding the puppy, but it should be carried out equally carefully. The biting action of the bitch sends the smooth muscle tissue into spasm sealing off the blood capillaries. Cutting the cord does not have the same effect. Hold the end of the cord nearest the puppy about 2 inches from its body, and then, with your right hand tear the cord exerting pressure towards the attached placenta, with your left hand remaining stationary. Never pull the cord overall, since this may result in an umbilical hernia. You can also cut the cord with a clean pair of scissors having previously tied it nearer the puppy;

The placentas are important because if one is retained within the bitch's body, it can cause a serious infection. It is possible for your veterinarian to detach any remaining placentas by means of an injection. If the bitch seems unable to settle down and continues straining, this is a sign that there may be a puppy stuck in the birth canal.

THE BIRTH PROCESS

A puppy in the process of being born is seen in the normal delivery position (**1**), emerging head first. A few minutes later the puppy is still emerging (**2**). The third and final stage of labor is the passing of the placenta which should follow within a quarter of an hour after the birth of each puppy (**3**). The umbilical cord is still connecting the mother and puppy and its greenish tinge is perfectly normal. The bitch may eat the afterbirth and will hopefully sever the umbilical cord herself. There is approximately a half hour interval between the birth of each puppy and they begin suckling almost immediately. In (**4**), one of the puppies is still wet and is being licked and cleaned by the mother.

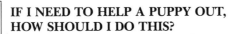

IF I NEED TO HELP A PUPPY OUT, HOW SHOULD I DO THIS?

It depends on the cause of the obstruction. Generally, assuming that the puppy is lying in a central position, you should gently and carefully pull it downwards with the bitch either standing or more usually lying on her side. Do not pull between contractions, but manipulate the puppy at this stage. If you are not making progress, contact your veterinarian immediately. Puppies are not as susceptible to oxygen starvation as human babies, but time is critical in the birth process and brain damage is likely to occur quite rapidly if they are deprived of oxygen.

WHAT NEEDS TO BE DONE AFTER THE BITCH HAS GIVEN BIRTH?

She will rest with her puppies and lick them clean. This in turn appears to stimulate them to suckle. Their food intake in the first couple of days following birth is critical to their later well-being. The *colostrum* provides them with protection against infections until their own immune systems are functioning properly. Weak puppies will probably be unable to suckle at this crucial stage and will cry as their body temperature falls, but the bitch will ignore them. Indeed, a healthy litter of puppies will be quite quiet unless they are cold. They are incapable of regulating their body temperature at this stage, so be sure that the room is kept warm, at least 70 °F, and if necessary, place a heating pad in the whelping box. These low wattage pads give off a gentle heat on their surface when the puppy's body is in contact with it. Always choose one of the metal designs rather than the similar models, which are made of plastic and can be broken by a bitch leaving the electrical cord exposed.

Puppies sleep together to conserve body heat; they space themselves out gradually as they develop the ability to thermoregulate. They will feed every couple of hours for the first week. Then the interval between feeds will rise to four hours or so. The hind teats are often preferred, and located by a sense of smell. Puppies are born blind; their eyes start to open when they are approaching two

Having been born, outside the whelping box, the first pup is shown to the mother (*left*) and then taken to the specially prepared and cozy box for its first experiences in a new world.

A bitch with a new-born litter of six Cocker Spaniels (*left*) should be left alone to recover from the ordeal of giving birth. She will lick them patiently, and they will start to suckle.

An Australian Cattle Dog bitch (*above*) is beginning to tire of continually feeding her offspring. As soon as they stop suckling, her milk supply will dry up.

weeks of age. Hearing takes a further week to develop effectively. At first, they will sleep for much of the time; they will begin to move about by the age of about two weeks. The mother controls their bodily functions early in life, stimulating both defecation and urination by licking the puppies and clearing up their deposits until they are three weeks old.

? HOW SHOULD I FEED MY BITCH WHO HAS JUST HAD PUPPIES?

Her food intake will increase as the litter grows. As a rough guide, she should be receiving 50 percent more food than usual in the first week, 100 percent more during the second week and then at least three times her normal ration from this point on as the puppies grow rapidly. Offer this in several meals through the day. It is also vital that the bitch receives an adequate intake of fluid to sustain her milk output. Water should be constantly available to her as always, but she can also be offered one of the special milk replacement foods that are used for rearing orphaned puppies. These are unlikely to precipitate diarrhea as quantities of cow's milk may because of the relatively high level of sugar present.

THE NEW PUPPIES

Suckling is vital to newborn puppies because their mother's milk contains antibodies that protect the puppies during the early weeks of life, until their own immunity develops.

? **ARE THERE ANY PROBLEMS THAT CAN OCCUR DURING THE REARING PERIOD?**

Dogs, in spite of their carnivorous nature, are not usually cannibalistic towards their offspring. Should the sire of the litter be on the premises, however, keep it away from the puppies lest he injure them. The male has no paternal instincts.

The bitch herself should be left quietly to recover from the trauma of giving birth, and to accustom herself to rearing her puppies. Watch her, though, in case she shows any sensitivity on a particular teat and refuses to let the puppies use it. The gland itself is likely to be the focus of a local infection, called *mastitis*, and will require antibiotic treatment to reduce the swelling and overcome the bacteria that are the likely cause.

Small breeds generally have relatively small litters, but exceptions do occur. Such bitches can suffer from the effects of calcium deficiency. This gives rise to the acute condition known under such names as *milk fever, eclampsia* and *puerperal tetany.* It can occur at any stage but it is most likely to develop from two weeks to a month after whelping, when milk production peaks. The bitch appears distressed and may start to ignore the puppies and refuse to eat.

One of the functions of calcium is to assist in muscular contraction, and the bitch will begin to stagger as her muscles are affected. Her temperature will rise, and if left untreated, she will start convulsing and collapse. Eclampsia can prove fatal, so rapid treatment is required at the earliest opportunity after the condition has been diagnosed. The response to an injection of a

LITTER SIZE ACCORDING TO BREED

Breed	Mean litter size	Breed	Mean litter size	Breed	Mean litter size
Airedale Terrier	7.6	Doberman	7.6	Norwegian Elkhound, black	4.8
Australian Terrier	5.0	English Foxhound	7.3	Pappillion	5.0
Basenji	5.5	English Setter	6.3	Pekingese	10.0
Beagle	5.6	English Springer Spaniel	6.0	Pinscher, miniature	3.4
Bedlington Terrier	5.6	Fox Terrier, smooth-hair	4.1	Pointer	6.7
Bernese Mountain Dog	5.8	Fox Terrier, wirehair	3.9	Pomeranian	2.0
Bloodhound	10.1	French Bulldog	5.8	Poodle, miniature	4.3
Boston Terrier	3.6	German Shepherd Dog	8.0	Poodle, standard	6.4
Boxer	6.4	Golden Retriever	8.1	Retriever	5.2
Brussels Griffon	4.0	Gordon Setter	7.5	Rottweiler	7.5
Bulldog	5.9	Greyhound	6.8	Samoyed	6.0
Bull Terrier	3.6	Irish Setter	7.2	St Bernard	8.5
Cairn Terrier	3.6	Kerry Blue Terrier	4.7	Schnauzer, giant	8.7
Chow	4.6	King Charles Spaniel	3.0	Schnauzer, standard	5.1
Cocker Spaniel	4.8	Labrador Retriever	7.8	Scottish Terrier	4.9
Collie	7.9	Lakeland Terrier	3.3	Shetland Sheepdog	4.0
Dachshund, smooth-hair	4.8	Lapland Dog	4.8	Shih Tzu	3.4
Dachshund, longhair	3.1	Manchester Terrier	4.7	Siberian Husky	5.9
Dachshund, wirehair	4.5	Mastiff	7.7	Welsh Corgi (Pembroke)	5.5
Dalmatian	5.8	Newfoundland	6.3	West Highland White Terrier	3.7
Dandie Dinmont Terrier	5.3	Norwegian Elkhound, gray	6.0	Whippet	4.4

The great variation in the litter size of dogs of different breeds is apparent from the figures in this chart. The biggest litter reported consisted of 23 puppies.

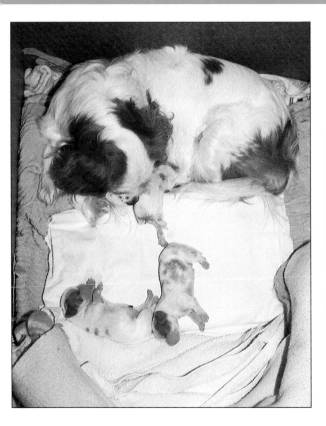

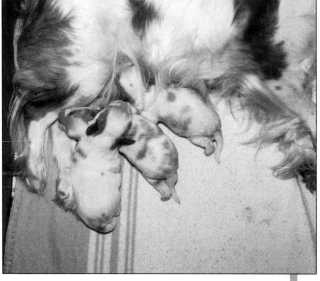

Newborn pups, 24 hours of age (*left*), are unable to see, hear or smell and rely on their sense of touch, feeding every two hours and sleeping in between. By the time they are one week old (*below*) they will be able to crawl around their nest and will burrow into anything soft and warm, even a human hand.

calcium compound administered by a veterinarian is likely to be equally speedy. There are considerable demands on the mother's supply of calcium both for the developing skeletal systems of the fetuses during pregnancy and then in milk production. Even if she makes a full recovery, it will be necessary to remove at least some of the puppies for hand-rearing or for fostering to another bitch with a smaller litter. Your veterinarian may be able to assist you in finding a suitable foster-parent. Bitches producing milk as the result of a pseudo-pregnancy can be satisfactory for this purpose.

? WHEN SHOULD THE WEANING PROCESS START?

It usually begins when the puppies are approximately three weeks of age. Do not be surprised if the bitch apparently vomits food which they then consume. This is natural behavior. Obtain one of the special canned puppy foods, which are normally highly palatable. Offer this on a saucer so you can assist them because some puppies are very reluctant to eat on their own at first. It may be necessary to feed them first by offering a little of the food on the end of a finger.

Let them smell the meat initially because they will be reluctant to consume it otherwise. The bitch's attitude towards the puppies will also change during subsequent weeks. She will leave them for longer periods and will be less keen to suckle them. This results in a lower output of milk causing the puppies to seek alternative food elsewhere.

Their first teeth will have started to emerge by the time they are six weeks old, as they begin to become independent. The puppies should be receiving four meals a day at this stage, with the first and last feeds of the day comprised of a milk-replacement food in the form of a powder mixed with water. Offer increasing quantities of the chosen balanced puppy food and augment the meat content of the diet with a little freshly cooked food. The precise amount will depend on the number of puppies. Feed them separately from the bitch to prevent her taking their food, or supervise their feeding. The frequency of feeding is gradually reduced; the milk-based feeds are eliminated when the puppy is about four months old, and by the age of six months, the young dog is receiving two meals daily. As a general guide, puppies require about twice as much food as an adult dog of the same weight.

? IF NECESSARY, CAN I HAND REAR THE PUPPIES?

It is possible to hand rear puppies successfully, but this is an extremely time-consuming process and fostering is generally preferable. Nevertheless, if the bitch has died or is otherwise incapacitated and unable to feed her litter (possibly following a Caesarian birth or an attack of eclampsia) and you wish to keep the puppies, there will be no other option. You will need a milk replacer and a suitable feeding bottle. Both should be available through a large pet store; it may be a good idea to acquire these items prior to the expected whelping of the bitch in case of an emergency. Mix the milk powder as directed and check the temperature. It should be at about 100 °F immediately prior to feeding. Any remaining milk after a feed is best discarded; the food should be prepared fresh on each occasion. If necessary, it may keep satisfactorily in a refrigerator for up to a day. Warm up the required volume to the correct temperature before use. Significant differences exist between a bitch's milk and the milk produced by other mammals, including humans. It is notably low in lactose and relatively high in protein and fat, as well as calcium and phosphorus. In a crisis situation, however, a human milk replacer can be used but it may cause diarrhea because of its high lactose content.

A newborn puppy (*below*) is most safely held using both hands to support its whole body.

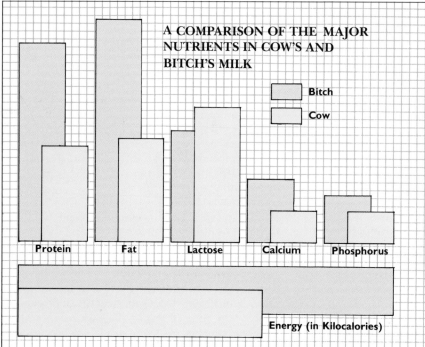

A COMPARISON OF THE MAJOR NUTRIENTS IN COW'S AND BITCH'S MILK

Bitch

Cow

Protein Fat Lactose Calcium Phosphorus

Energy (in Kilocalories)

In terms of the major nutrients, milk from the puppies' mother contains approximately twice as much energy value as cow's milk, as is apparent from the graph (*left*). If puppies require supplementary feeding they should be given a specially formulated bitch-milk substitute. Cow's milk is detrimental to the growth and development of a puppy and may cause severe diarrhea.

Starting to feed your puppy solids may require some encouragement at first, by allowing him to lick food from your finger (above).

It may be preferable to feed the puppies individually to insure that they all have an adequate share and that there are no squabbles among the siblings (right).

THE FIRST FEW WEEKS

Feeding must be carried out slowly. Let the puppy feed at its own pace, thus minimizing the risk of fluid being introduced inadvertently to its lungs and causing fatal pneumonia. The puppies will need to be fed very frequently during the early weeks of their lives — every two hours from about 6.00 am to midnight with a further couple of feeds during the night. Once the puppy appears to have had enough, wipe around the mouth with a moistened piece of cotton and then wipe the rear quarters. This mimics the licking behavior of the bitch and encourages the puppy to relieve itself. The orphaned puppy on its own runs the risk of becoming chilled without its mother and siblings to curl up with. Place a warm but covered hot water bottle in its bed, in addition to a heating pad. Further heat can be supplied by an infra-red lamp suspended above the bed if necessary; choose one of the models designed for use with livestock. These are more durable and emit heat and no light so the puppy can settle down as night falls. Check the temperature with a thermometer and if possible include a thermostat in conjunction with the light

so that there is no risk of the puppy becoming too hot. Start off with a temperature about 85 °F, and gradually lower this over successive weeks to 70 °F. If the temperature becomes too low, the puppy will start whining. If it gets too hot, the puppy will also become distressed. Allow for a cooler area in the bed so the puppy can decide where it feels most comfortable. Under normal circumstances, puppies will sleep together in a group to maintain their body temperature and at first they make few sounds — apart from an occasional grunt of contentment. Crying means that the puppy is either hungry or cold.

Cleanliness will be a vital factor in the successful hand rearing of orphaned puppies, especially if they did not receive any colostrum from the bitch. Always clean out the feeding utensils very thoroughly between feeds, using one of the proprietary sterilizing fluids or tablets which dissolve in water following a thorough wash with detergent. Do not forget to rinse the detergent off the feeder and then rinse again prior to use. Although hand rearing is a time-consuming process, ultimately, it is rewarding and worthwhile.

BREEDING PROBLEMS

Sexuality is the key to many of dogs' anti-social behavioral traits. The decision to "de-sex" a dog is debatable but, it does curtail many problems in both male and female dogs.

? WHAT SYMPTOMS SHOULD I WATCH FOR IF MY BITCH DOES DEVELOP PYOMETRA?

This disorder typically affects bitches over five years of age. It can be difficult to detect in onset, but it will be linked to periods of heat and will usually become apparent during the second month following the previous season. The bitch may stop eating and drink more than normal, a reflection of an increased urinary output. Vomiting can also occur, and the abdomen will swell noticeably in size, especially if there is only a small discharge from the vulva. This is sometimes described as a *closed pyometra* and indicates a swelling of the uterus with most unpleasant fluid contents. If you suspect that your bitch is developing pyometra, contact your veterinarian as soon as possible. Surgery to remove the infected uterus and the ovaries is generally the only satisfactory treatment. Your veterinarian may wish to confirm the diagnosis by taking X-rays. Pyometra is a serious condition (with the bitch becoming toxemic), but a full recovery is likely if surgery is carried out and there are no complications.

? I HAVE A LITTER OF PUPPIES OF A BREED THAT NORMALLY HAS THE TAILS DOCKED. WHAT IS THE PURPOSE OF THIS OPERATION, AND WHEN SHOULD IT BE CARRIED OUT?

Tail docking entails the removal of part of the tail and was originally carried out to save a hunting dog's tail from injury when it was running through undergrowth. Since then, docking has been incorporated into the breed standards of

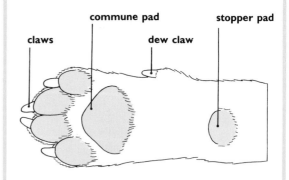

DEW CLAWS

commune pad

claws

dew claw

stopper pad

The dew claws are vestigial digits that do not come into contact with the surface and their removal depends to some extent on the breed concerned. However, in some breeds the standard may demand the dew claws are retained and this can be to the dog's detriment.

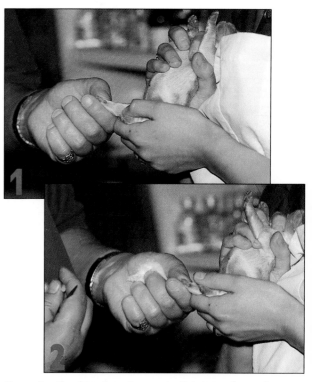

Removing the dew claws is a practical and sensible operation (*above*) and should be performed by a veterinarian, ideally when the puppy is between four and seven days old. In (**1**) the dew claw can be seen prior to the operation and (**2**), after the operation.

numerous breeds, and exhibitors are usually forced to submit their dogs to this unnecessary mutilation if they wish to show them. The amount of tail that has to be removed is also specified; for example the Rottweiler has the majority of its tail amputated leaving just a single vertebra, while the Airedale keeps most of the tail with only the tip being removed.

If you have to have puppies' tails docked, be sure this is carried out properly by asking a veterinarian to undertake the task. Do not be surprised if the veterinarian refuses to do it.

? DOES THE REMOVAL OF DEW CLAWS FIT INTO THE SAME CATEGORY AS TAIL DOCKING?

No. The dew claws are vestigial remains of the digit equivalent to our thumb or big toe and can cause injury and pain to a dog unfortunate enough to be caught by one. Unlike the tail, which can be used to keep flies off the dog's body, for example, the dew claws have no clear function. It is the hind dew claws which are particularly dangerous for the dog, but in some breeds, including the Briard and Pyrenean Mountain Dog, the official standard demands double dew claws on the two rear legs and in a show dog these cannot be removed.

There is a further danger associated with intact dew claws. This relates to the claw itself. Since this claw does not extend to the ground, there is no wear on its surface and it can rapidly become

The cropping of ears is unnecessary — only serving to give a dog a more ferocious appearance — and illegal in some countries, such as the United Kingdom. Dogs like this Boxer (*below*) that have had their ears clipped are rarely seen nowadays.

overgrown and curl around to impinge on or even penetrate into the flesh of the pad. Keep a close watch on hind dew claws. They can be removed in puppies at an early age with minimum problems. Speak to your veterinarian about this prior to the birth of a litter. Surgical removal is also possible in older dogs and may be inevitable following injury, but it is a more troublesome operation.

? I AM WORRIED ABOUT MY BITCH COMING INTO HEAT AND BEING ACCIDENTALLY MATED. IS IT POSSIBLE TO GIVE HER A CHEMICAL CONTRACEPTIVE?

Yes. There are chemical means both for delaying the onset of a heat and preventing it from occurring when early signs are apparent. Discuss these and other options with your veterinarian when you take your bitch for her inoculations. The method may be influenced to some extent by the circumstances. If you have made vacation plans, you will not want to take your bitch with you while she is in heat nor will a kennel want to take her; a hormonal treatment will be necessary. The *progestogens* are one group of compounds used for this purpose. They are administered either in pill form or by injection. It is quite possible for the bitch to be mated successfully at her next heat and produce healthy puppies with no side effects. These artificial hormones work by mimicking the action of the natural hormone progesterone in inhibiting the secretion of another hormone, estrogen which is required for estrus itself to begin.

There is no reason for the customary docking of certain dogs' tails, and this Boxer (*above*) — a breed that often has the tail docked — has an intact tail.

MY BITCH WAS MATED AS WE HAD HOPED BY OUR NEIGHBOR'S DOG. IS THERE ANY RISK OF HER MATING WITH OTHER DOGS IF WE START TAKING HER OUT NOW?

Yes. After a planned series of matings, do not let your bitch out because other males will inevitably be attracted by her. Such liaisons could actually result in a mixed litter of puppies with different fathers. The spermatozoa may survive for as long as a week in the bitch's reproductive tract. There is no risk of any effects of a previous mating being apparent at the next heat in spite of the popular belief that a pedigreed bitch that is mated by a mongrel dog will be affected over successive litters.

MY MALE DOG PERSISTS IN MOUNTING MY LEG, ESPECIALLY WHEN I SIT DOWN. IS THIS USUAL?

Behavior of this type is relatively common in young male dogs and should be a passing phase. It may be that the dog was weaned rather early in life and did not socialize sufficiently with his littermates. Whether or not this is a true explanation is unclear. Such behavior is not just confined to male dogs, but may also occur in bitches. It is most unusual for dogs to show no interest in each other; when a bitch is in heat, normal mating is almost certain to occur.

If the dog does not desist, isolate it as soon as it starts such behavior. The situation should improve within a week or so when the dog realizes that it will be ostracized whenever it exhibits such behavior. Alternatively, castration can prove the answer. But not every case responds to it — possibly because such behavior has become ingrained. The administration of progestogens can lead to an improvement if surgery alone does not produce a remission.

I AM CONSIDERING HAVING MY BITCH NEUTERED. WHAT DOES THIS ENTAIL?

This operation, known technically as *ovariohysterectomy,* results in the removal of both the ovaries and the uterus and is usually described as spaying. It is much more invasive than castration because the abdominal cavity has to be opened via either the flank or the midline of the abdomen on its lower surface. The approach will vary, depending on the bitch concerned. When a flank incision is used, the coat color immediately surrounding the site of the flank will probably appear paler than the rest of the coat for life, but the small scar will be obscured. The wound heals quickly, and the external stitches (sutures) should be removed by your veterinarian about 10 days after surgery. Keep an eye on the incision, however, in case any sutures break prematurely, revealing internal tissue. Contact your veterinarian as soon as possible in this event.

After the operation, your bitch should be kept quiet for a few days and should not be encouraged to leap or jump around. It should be exercized only on a leash. After spaying, the bitch will not undergo heats or pseudo-pregnancies. Spaying, like castration, is irreversible. Spaying is usually carried out during the period of the anestrus phase. Possible side effects to keep in mind are a slight risk of incontinence later in life and, more significantly, a noticeable increase in weight. This is also likely to happen to male dogs that have been castrated, and their diet will have to be modified accordingly. The coat may also become coarse. It will be several months before the hair covers the scar left by the operation.

It should be fairly evident when a male dog has been castrated (bearing in mind the possibility of a cryptorchid), but in a bitch, evidence of spaying can be harder to see unless the skin is palpated to reveal the scar tissue beneath. This may be useful with a bitch whose history is unknown, and it saves the bitch from being anesthetized unnecessarily.

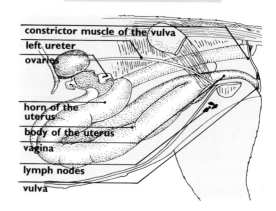

constrictor muscle of the vulva
left ureter
ovaries
horn of the uterus
body of the uterus
vagina
lymph nodes
vulva

This operation is technically an ovariohysterectomy and entails the removal of both uterus and ovaries. It is ideally performed in the period between heats (anestrus). The abdominal cavity has to be opened either at the flank or through the midline of the ventral surface. The wound heals quickly and stitches are normally removed about 10 days afterwards.

CASTRATION

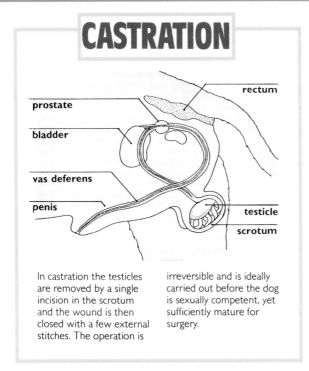

In castration the testicles are removed by a single incision in the scrotum and the wound is then closed with a few external stitches. The operation is irreversible and is ideally carried out before the dog is sexually competent, yet sufficiently mature for surgery.

 I AM THINKING OF HAVING MY MALE DOG NEUTERED. WHAT DOES THIS OPERATION ENTAIL, AND WILL IT LEAD TO ANY CHANGE IN HIS TEMPERAMENT?

Owners may be advised in certain circumstances to have their male dogs neutered as a means of curbing certain behavioral problems, notably wandering. Studies suggest that although it is not successful in every case, about 90 percent of dogs show less desire to wander after neutering, and their sexual libido is curbed. This operation may not discourage a dog from mating, however, if it was sexually experienced beforehand. Other behavioral difficulties of sexual origin, such as uncontrollable scent markings with urine around the home, may also respond to surgery. Neutering the male dog, described as *castration*, is a relatively straightforward operation, particularly when carried out in a dog approaching sexual maturity. It is not reversible, however, since both testes are removed through a cut in the scrotal sac.

MY DOG APPEARS TO HAVE ONLY ONE TESTICLE. SURELY THIS IS NOT CORRECT?

The two testicles develop within the abdomen and then descend via the inguinal canal to the scrotum. It is believed that body temperature in mammals is too high for the process of sperm formation, known as *spermatogenesis*, to take place inside the body so the testes are held in an external sac. Incidentally, the elephant is a notable exception to this generalization! In the case of a puppy, both testicles should be present in the scrotum by six months of age. Some breeds, notably the Yorkshire Terrier, show an increased incidence of the condition known as *cryptorchidism*, when one or both testicles fail to descend as normal. It is important that you seek medical advice; exploratory surgery will be necessary to locate the other testicle. If left inside the body, the testicle may cause a specific kind of tumor, described as a *sertoli cell tumor*, which will be malignant. In order to resolve the problem completely, your veterinarian may recommend removal of both testicles at the same time, thus completing castration. Since cryptorchidism may sometimes be inherited, affected dogs should not be used for breeding, although an implant of testosterone may cure the dog.

I'VE JUST SEEN MY BITCH BEING MATED. SHE RAN OUT ACCIDENTALLY AND I DON'T WANT HER TO HAVE PUPPIES AT THIS TIME. IS THERE ANYTHING THAT CAN BE DONE TO PREVENT THIS?

Bitches tend to wander in search of mates when in heat, and there is nothing you can do once the liaison has formed. Indeed, trying to separate two dogs that are mating can result in serious injury to one or both of the participants. Furthermore, ejaculation of the spermatozoa occurs very early during the process, and any interference would probably be unsuccessful. A possible, safe means of disengaging the dogs may be to throw a bucket of water over them, but this is rarely on hand at the crucial moment.

Telephone your veterinarian as soon as possible during office hours and explain what happened. Conception can be prevented if an estrogen injection is given within a couple of days after the mating takes place. Time is important. Unfortunately, although effective, estrogen will of course prolong the estrus phase and increase the risk of other dogs being attracted to your bitch. If you have no plans to breed from the bitch in the future, it may be preferable to have her spayed as soon as possible. This will prevent the problem recurring. The operation removes the embarrassment and trouble associated with heat periods and unwanted litters which often lead to an increase in the stray dog population.

THE ELDERLY DOG

3

As time passes, so the dog will begin to show signs of aging. In most cases however, dogs remain reasonably active up until the end. Modern medicines have done much to relieve many of the common troublesome symptoms of old age, although clearly it is not possible to cure certain ailments such as a deterioration in kidney function, diabetes and other metabolic disorders. Regular veterinary check-ups are therefore likely to be increasingly necessary at this stage in the dog's life, to insure that all possible care can be given and medication adjusted according to need. However, an elderly dog will still provide you with years of pleasure.

The fading color on the head of this Golden Retriever (*right*) is a typical sign of aging in a dog. Other more insidious and serious problems may be harder to detect in their initial stages — kidney failure and incontinence are common medical problems.

THE SENIOR CITIZEN

The problems of age in dogs, as in humans, are usually insidious in onset. A range of diseases — cardiac, renal and tumorous — become an increasing danger.

? HOW LONG CAN I EXPECT MY DOG TO LIVE?

As a general rule, the bigger breeds tend to have a shorter lifespan than their smaller cousins. Giant breeds such as the Irish Wolfhound are unlikely to live more than 10 years, but some small terriers and toy dogs may live until well into their teens. There are of course exceptions to every rule, and dogs have lived into their thirties. While it is sometimes said that every year of our lives is equivalent to seven years in the life of a dog, this is essentially untrue. It arose from the idea that humans lived for the biblical "three score years and ten," or 70 years, and that dogs had an average lifespan of 10 years.

? WHAT ARE THE VISIBLE SIGNS OF AGING?

Aging is a slow process, even in the dog, and changes tend to be gradual. They are not necessarily evident at a casual glance. The coat color is likely to become paler over successive shedding; the Golden Labrador, for example, becomes whitish rather than golden, while its black counterpart becomes paler around the muzzle with silvery white hairs evident. You are likely to notice a decrease in activity in your dog; it will not want to walk long distances and will be content to potter along slowly rather than racing along like a young puppy. Its teeth, after a lifetime of service, may be showing signs of wear, and the dog may appear reluctant to chew as it used to do when younger.

Obesity is a common adjunct to aging, because the dog's level of activity declines, but it often receives the same quantity of food it ate as a young

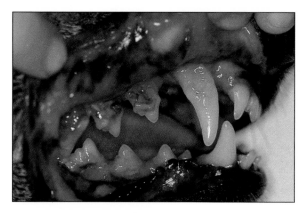

INTRODUCING A NEWCOMER

It is important for the owner to be aware of the pack order between two dogs in the same family. Trouble is more likely to arise if the owner gives more attention to and favors the new dog as the natural

order is upset (**1**). The dominant member of the pair — the older, established individual of the household — will naturally defend his position by attacking the newcomer (**2**). To

counteract this natural behavior, the owner should show attention to the dominant, older dog so that the position of both dogs will be defined and the hierarchy accepted (**3**).

adult dog. Obesity can create and worsen other problems of aging, such as *osteoarthrosis* (a loss of the cartilage lining certain joints). Failing senses may also be apparent, with a decline in eyesight being perhaps most noticeable. Deafness is also common but may not be detected by owners because they just assume their dog is becoming more stubborn and disobedient in old age. But dogs are adaptable by nature, and an individual that is perhaps almost totally blind can live quite well without injuring itself in familiar surroundings.

Constipation may also afflict the older dog as the gut tone declines. This can be overcome by the administration of mineral oil. In certain instances, as the *uptake mechanisms* in the gut begin to fail, the feces become more liquid, and diarrhea results. Urinary incontinence, often associated with kidney failure, can also accompany the aging process, and treatment can prove difficult.

WHAT CAN I DO IF MY DOG LOSES HIS TEETH?

Certain breeds are more prone to dental decay than others. Yorkshire Terriers, for example, often lose most of their teeth when they are in middle-age. Dental decay may be linked to diet; soft diets based on home-prepared foods or on cans of dog food, tend to encourage the build-up of tartar on the teeth. Tartar contains bacteria which cause both tooth decay and gum disease. It is a good idea to provide hard items, such as dog biscuits, on a regular basis to reduce the tartar accumulation. The teeth can also be cleaned with a special canine toothpaste. An older dog that has lost the majority of its teeth will still be able to eat adequately if offered soft foods. In any event, dogs do not use their teeth for chewing purposes but for catching prey and tearing strips of flesh that can be swallowed whole. Neither of these functions are of significance for the pet dog.

Dental problems such as this build-up of tartar which has led to gum disease (*left*) tend to afflict dogs in the older age bracket. These teeth will have to be cleaned by a veterinarian, with the dog under anesthetic.

In old age as synthesis of melanin is reduced the coat and nose color become paler and as in this Beagle (*right*), white hairs begin to show, particularly around the muzzle.

WHAT SKELETAL PROBLEMS MAY MY DOG ENCOUNTER IN OLD AGE?
These are likely to be degenerative conditions such as *osteoarthrosis*, a loss of the cartilage lining certain joints, especially those of the hip and stifle. This affects bigger dogs in particular, and causes lameness, which is most marked after a period of rest. The condition usually improves following movement, but some medication to relieve the pain in bad cases may be indicated. If the dog is overweight, the problem is worse because the joints have to carry a greater burden than normal.

Slipped disks are more likely to occur in a slightly younger group of dogs, but the weakness remains throughout an affected individual's life. The disks themselves occupy the intervertebral spaces between the vertebrae and prevent friction — they act as shock-absorbers. If there is a weakness in their outer layer, however, the inner core of the disk expands and presses against the spinal cord. This in turn causes considerable pain, and results in paralysis of either the front or hind legs depending on whether the disk concerned is in the neck or towards the tail. It is a very common complaint in Dachshunds and may be related to their long bodies. Dachshunds should be discouraged from jumping on chairs or climbing stairs as these activities can predispose them to slipped disks.

Treatment tends to be supportive. The dog is kept as quiet as possible and confined to a small area so that it cannot injure itself further. Medical treatment decreases the inflammation and eases the pain. Given the sensitivity of the neck region of the Dachshund, especially in the older dog, it makes sense to use a harness rather than a collar to remove stress from a sensitive part of the dog's anatomy.

 DO MANY OLD DOGS DIE OF CANCER?
The incidence of tumors in dogs averages about four in a thousand and about one-third of these are likely to prove malignant (cancerous). Older dogs are most likely to develop both benign and malignant tumors. The benign tumor is relatively slow-growing and does not spread and invade other tissues. As a result, it can be removed fairly easily (depending on its location in the body). New tumors will not develop from it in other parts of the body, a process associated with malignant tumors and known as *metastasis*.

The skin is the most common site for tumors in the dog, and this facilitates early detection. Other likely sites include the mammary glands of bitches. In this instance, studies have revealed that bitches spayed before their first heat are 200 times less likely to develop such tumors than bitches

Dogs with short legs and a long body such as Dachshunds (*left*), Beagles and Basset Hounds are prone to suffering from occasional back pain and sometimes even a slipped disk. This is due to the vertebral canal enclosing the spinal cord being made up of a number of vertebrae, each joined to the next by a flexible pad — the so-called intervertebral disk, consisting of outer fibrous layers and an inner gelatinous area. If the spine is flexed too vigorously, especially in an older, long-backed dog, a prolapsed or 'slipped' disk may occur, as the soft centre of the intervetebral disk bursts up into the spinal canal, causing serious injury.

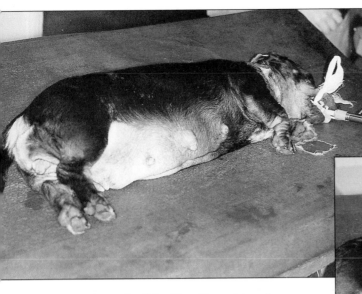

The large lump around the nipple of this ten year old Dachshund (*left*) is a typical sign of a mammary tumor and the dog is having to undergo surgery to remove it. Stitches show the site of the tumor along the same mammary chain (*below*) and the chances of survival for the dog increase the sooner the lump is removed.

neutered later in life. To offset this of course, possibly one in ten young bitches may develop urinary incontinence later in life because of spaying. Older dogs are increasingly susceptible to tumors in these two locations, but most of these tumors are not malignant. The incidence of major malignant tumors in dogs appears to peak between seven and ten years of age. These afflict the skeleton and the lymphatic system. Large breeds are most likely to have bone cancer.

? HOW CAN CANCER BE TREATED?

This depends largely on the type, size and locality of the tumor. It may be possible to operate and excise the tumor, but there is always a risk of recurrence, particularly with a malignancy. It may recur at the same site or elsewhere in the body. A refinement of the surgical approach is *cryosurgery* in which a liquid gas such as nitrogen at a very low temperature is applied to the affected tissue. The intense cold kills the cells and thus obviates the need for any incision. The area round the tumor is masked off to protect it while the probe is being used.

Cryosurgery has a number of advantages over traditional surgery, particularly in the case of skin tumors. The patient does not have to be fully anesthetized in some instances, and this can be a distinct advantage with an old dog in declining health. Since there is no bleeding, there is less likelihood in the case of a malignant tumor that cells will spread around the body to set up secondary tumors elsewhere. Using cryosurgery it is also possible to treat areas of the body, around the anus for example, that would bleed quite profusely if attempts were made to cut away the tumor. There is also less risk of an infection following surgery.

The major drawback to cryosurgery is that the tissue that has been frozen does not drop off at once, and waiting for this to occur may be unpleasant. It may be necessary to repeat the treatment if some of the diseased tissue remains unaffected. This applies also in skin conditions such as warts where there is little fluid present. The ice-crystals formed will disrupt the cellular structure of living tissue after freezing. It is now accepted practice to inject warts with water to achieve the best effect.

Cryosurgery does not provide a means of treating every tumor, especially those within the body. Here radiation therapy can lead to a remission, often in conjunction with chemotherapy which entails the use of drugs. The side-effects of these drugs are not usually as unpleasant in dogs as in humans. If radiation therapy is not available in your area, you may have to travel several times to a veterinary school doing research into radiation therapy to obtain this treatment.

? MY DOG HAS BEEN HOUSEBROKEN SINCE PUPPYHOOD, BUT RECENTLY HAS STARTED TO WET INDOORS AGAIN. COULD THIS BE A SIGN OF OLD AGE?

It may be linked to the kidneys. If the dog is drinking more, more urine will be produced, and the bladder will need to be emptied more frequently. For this reason, it is not unusual for older dogs to soil their quarters overnight while remaining clean for the rest of the day when someone is on hand to let them out to urinate more frequently. Keep a close check on the amount of fluid that your dog is consuming and inform your veterinarian. Note whether urine trickles out of the vulva in the case of a bitch, especially without its knowledge. This will stain the coat below the vulva. Be more responsive to your dog's requests to go out. Try to leave it alone in the home for only short periods, and let it out beforehand to empty its bladder.

? IS HEART FAILURE A COMMON CAUSE OF DEATH IN ELDERLY DOGS?

Dogs rarely succumb to coronary thrombosis (a condition in which blood clots occlude the pulmonary arteries nourishing the heart). Similarly, fatty deposits within the circulatory system are also uncommon. But the incidence of heart disease in elderly dogs is quite high and relates to the valvular structure of this vital organ. The four chambers of the heart are separated by valves, and left-sided failure is most common. The mitral valve becomes thickened so that blood does not leave the heart as usual. The actual symptoms of valvular disease vary. When the mitral valve is affected, the dog is likely to cough frequently and to tire easily when out for a walk. Coughing is most apparent either after exercise or at night and may be coupled with difficulty in breathing.

In the case of right-sided failure, the tricuspid valve is affected. Fluid builds up in the tissues because of increased pressure in the circulatory system from blood unable to enter the heart at the usual rate. Organs such as the spleen and liver also become engorged with blood and swell in size. These changes can be detected when your veterinarian examines the dog. If both valves are failing, a combination of symptoms will be seen.

Once the condition has been diagnosed, it can be stabilized with drugs, and you should see an improvement in your dog's condition. The cardiac glycosides, of which digitalis is best known, control the heart rate. By slowing its pace and improving its contractibility, they increase cardiac output. Diuretic drugs remove excessive fluid and sodium salt from the blood via the kidneys and thus decrease the pressure on the heart itself. The initial dose of drugs will be higher than the maintenance dose, which will then be administered throughout the dog's life, especially if the dog is seriously ill. This may result in symptoms of toxicity such as vomiting. If you are concerned, contact your veterinarian.

? THE VETERINARIAN TREATING MY DOG FOR BONE CANCER HAS RECOMMENDED PARTIAL AMPUTATION OF THE AFFECTED LEG. IS THIS FAIR, AS HE HAS ALWAYS BEEN SUCH AN ACTIVE DOG?

The choice ultimately has to be yours in this kind of situation, but you can rely on the sympathetic and understanding support of your veterinarian. Surprising as it may seem, dogs do adapt quite well to life on three legs and can live a relatively normal existence without appearing distressed. The idea may be abhorrent to you, however, and if so, you should opt to have your dog put to sleep before the malignancy spreads further within the body. Before deciding, ask your veterinarian if you can see a former patient that has undergone such surgery. This will give you a better idea of what to expect, and you can talk to the owner who, like you, would have been equally concerned at the outset. The surgery itself is unlikely to result in

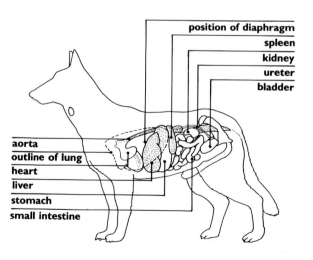

The position of the thoracic and abdominal organs in a dog.

position of diaphragm
spleen
kidney
ureter
bladder

aorta
outline of lung
heart
liver
stomach
small intestine

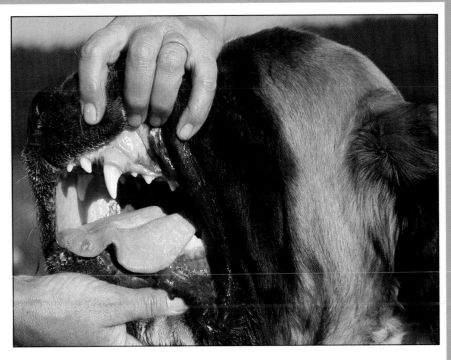

A bluish tinge on a dog's tongue (*right*) may be an indication of a kidney failure, typical of an older dog.

complications, but when you take your dog out for walks afterward, be prepared for strange looks or comments from other people.

❓ MY DOG IS SUFFERING FROM CHRONIC KIDNEY FAILURE. IS THIS JUST PART OF THE AGING PROCESS?

All dogs are afflicted to a greater or lesser extent by kidney failure in old age. This is a progressive condition, and one of the first signs of it is the dog's foul-smelling breath (often linked with bad teeth). The body has a high reserve of functioning kidney tissue, but once the level falls to only 30 percent of the total available, kidney or renal failure follows and the waste products of body metabolism that are normally filtered out of the body by this route remain in the blood. Various infectious causes of chronic renal failure exist including both *infectious canine hepatitis* and *leptospirosis*. Damage from these diseases at an early age will become more noticeable later in life.

Your dog will drink more fluid and urinate more often. In order to diagnose the condition and assess its severity, the veterinarian may want to have a urine sample for testing. This can be collected in a broad plastic saucer such as those used for potted plants in the home. These are easier and more practical to use than a bottle. The large surface areas means that at least some of the urine will be collected. And, in any case, a large volume of urine

is not necessary. Once you have the sample, transfer it to a clean, dry, screw-top container. Never use jars that have previously held jam because any remaining deposits of sugar are likely to interfere with the results.

In cases of chronic renal failure, there is no effective curative treatment. But you can modify the diet in order to improve your dog's state of health. Special canned foods are available from your veterinarian for this purpose. The protein level of the diet needs to be reduced overall, while the protein itself must be of higher biological value in terms of its amino acid content. Eggs, for example, are a useful source of such protein. Vitamin B supplementation may also be required since these water-soluble compounds will be lost in increasing quantities via the kidneys. A deficiency of nicotinic acid will cause the tongue to turn blackish in color, and this is a typical symptom of long-standing renal degeneration. Other changes, especially in the skeletal system, may occur in cases of chronic renal failure because a form of vitamin D known as 1,25 DHCC is synthesized in the kidneys and it acts on the intestines to regulate calcium absorption there. It also exerts an influence on calcium stores within the body itself. A similar compound which stimulates the bone marrow also originates in the kidneys, and thus anemia and resulting complications can also arise from kidney failure.

THE BIG SLEEP

If your dog is suffering and there is not hope of recovery, it is kinder for you to end your pet's misery and have him or her put to sleep. This is invariably a traumatic decision.

? HOW WILL MY DOG BE PUT TO SLEEP?

The usual method involves the administration of a barbiturate by injection into a vein. It is quick and effective and mimics the procedure used when an intravenous barbiturate is given for anesthetic purposes but a stronger drug is used. Within seconds, the dog will be unconscious, and its heart stops almost immediately. With a dog that is known to be aggressive, a strong sedative in pill form may be given in meat beforehand. The process can be carried out efficiently after this medication has taken effect.

After you reach the decision, arrange a time with your veterinarian to leave your dog at his office and say farewell. While you can stay to the end, it is usually preferable from everyone's viewpoint, including the dog's, if this unpleasant task is carried out with minimum fuss. Dogs are very sensitive to the mood of those around them and will detect the emotion on this occasion. This could cause them to be more difficult. For this reason, it is better to have the task carried out at the veterinarian's office than at home.

? WHAT WILL HAPPEN TO THE BODY OF MY DOG AFTERWARD?

This will depend on your instructions. Many owners request that the veterinarian arrange the disposal of the body. Alternatively, it may be possible to arrange a private cremation. In some areas, you can purchase a plot at a pet cemetery, and the organization concerned may arrange burial and a headstone if required. It is not always possible to bury your dog in your yard because of local laws. If you do opt for this method, make sure that the grave is at least three feet in depth to deter scavengers such as foxes that might otherwise be attracted to the carcass.

? MY MOTHER'S DOG WAS PUT TO SLEEP SEVERAL WEEKS AGO. SHE STILL SEEMS VERY UPSET BY THIS LOSS. HOW CAN I HELP HER OUT OF THIS DEPRESSION?

The loss of a dog can be a devastating emotional blow, especially for people living alone with no other form of companionship. Indeed, it can be like losing a close relative. But the grieving process when a relative dies is recognized by society while the death of a dog passes largely unnoticed, except

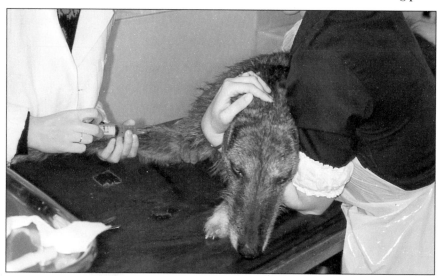

The decision to have a dog put to sleep can be difficult and the advice of your veterinarian may be helpful at this time. The actual process is painless — an intravenous injection of barbiturate being administered by the veterinarian (*left*) — and the dog loses consciousness within seconds. Parting with a pet dog is likely to prove traumatic for young and old alike and acquiring another dog may help alleviate the sense of loss, even though the newcomer cannot replace the previous dog directly.

There are plots that can be acquired as a final resting place for your faithful dog (*right*). Alternatively, your veterinarian will be able to arrange for a cremation or, you may wish to bury your pet in your backyard, in which case a deep grave of at least three feet will be necessary.

by the person directly affected. Grief in this instance is not usually expressed and builds up because the person is unable to unburden his or her sense of loss. Try to persuade your mother to talk about her lost pet. This can be therapeutic.

It may be that another dog would help, but be prepared for the comment that it could never take the place of her previous dog. Be positive — tell her that a new dog would not substitute directly for her other dog but be an individual in its own right. Given time, your mother is highly likely to accept a new dog with enthusiasm. If she feels that she cannot cope with another dog, suggest that she have another pet such as a parakeet. The positive benefits of owning a pet are becoming increasingly appreciated, and in some countries such as France, dog ownership is a right for all citizens, embodied in the constitution.

 HOW SHOULD I EXPLAIN TO MY CHILDREN THAT OUR DOG HAS BEEN PUT TO SLEEP?

This depends to some extent on the age of your children; it may be easiest to explain it by saying that the family dog went to sleep and will not wake up again. Children are often very upset by the death of a pet. Lacking the acquired reserve of most adults, they express their deep grief openly by crying and gradually come to terms with their sense of loss. The acquisition of another dog may also be helpful in overcoming this feeling.

 HOW SHOULD I DECIDE WHEN THE TIME HAS COME FOR MY DOG TO BE PUT TO SLEEP?

After a lifetime's companionship, it will be a difficult decision. Although your veterinarian can guide you, the ultimate responsibility must rest with you. Clearly, you do not want your dog to suffer unnecessarily when there is no hope of recovery. The decision may also be influenced by your personsal circumstances. In the case of a paraplegic dog unable to stand on its own, you may be able to obtain one of the special dog carts available to assist paralyzed dogs. The hindquarters are fitted to the cart and the forelegs, functioning as usual, pull them along. Not all dogs are happy with these attachments. And you may not be in a position to provide the extra attention that a dog of this type needs. Or you may find the sight of your dog in this state distressing. Under these circumstances, consider euthanasia.

General guidelines must revolve around the normal daily habits of your dog. Can it walk? Is it able to eat and drink properly? Is it continent? Does it still appear to enjoy life? These are the type of questions that you must honestly ask yourself before arriving at your decision.

If you do opt for euthanasia, it should be carried out by a veterinarian. Do not be surprised or upset if you are asked to sign a consent form. This transfers the legal right of deciding your animal's future to your veterinarian.

SECTION 2
UNDERSTANDING YOUR DOG'S AILMENTS

GENERAL HEALTH CARE

Modern advances in canine health care have meant that it is now possible to prevent the occurrence of the major fatal canine diseases, by means of regular inoculations. Safe anesthetics and sophisticated equipment also mean that surgical procedures can be undertaken, with minimum risk, so that the dog's life expectancy is probably greater than ever before. There are dangers however — in the home and on the road. Many dogs die each year from collisions with vehicles. Good training and supervision on the part of the dog's owner are thus vital parts of a health care program, apart from the veterinarian's direct involvement.

Modern nursing techniques and sophisticated veterinary techniques enable the successful treatment of most canine ailments or accidents (*right*).

YOUR VET

It is not difficult to find a veterinarian in most areas, and soon after a new dog is acquired, it is a good idea to visit the local surgery, so inoculations can be given if necessary, and a check up carried out.

? HOW CAN I TELL IF MY DOG IS ILL AND IN NEED OF VETERINARY ATTENTION?

The key indicators are likely to be the dog's appetite and drinking habits, as well as its general alertness and desire to exercise. When you take your dog to a veterinarian, go with a written list of symptoms that are worrying you and the length of time they have lasted. The veterinarian may also want to know the date of the bitch's last heat or whether she has been neutered, how long you have had her, and if she has been inoculated. Some of this information may be available to the veterinarian if you have made previous visits, but have it on hand. Your veterinarian will probably ask you questions before carrying out an examination of the dog. This is sometimes referred to as "taking the history of the case". Be precise as far as possible. If your dog has been drinking more water, specify the amount by saying that it now consumes X quarts over the course of a day. It is very difficult for a veterinarian to gain a meaningful impression if you say that the dog empties two bowls without telling him or her the volume of the bowls concerned! Keep a watch on your dog when it relieves itself. You will then be able to say whether or not it has any difficulty in urinating or defecating.

? DOES IT MATTER WHETHER I GO TO THE SAME VETERINARIAN EVERY TIME?

In the larger cities, many veterinary practices are comprised of a group of veterinarians rather than a single one. There are obvious advantages to this system. Duty hours can be rotated, and veterinarians with particular interests can

The eyes, nose, mouth and ears are all good indicators of the overall state of health of your dog. The eyes should be clear and bright and the nose should also be free of any discharge or redness (*above*); a mucus discharge may be an early sign of any upper respiratory infection or even distemper. The mouth and gums should be pink (*center left*); bad breath being a sign of tooth decay or gum disease. A dog with severe periodontal disease will be prone to dribble. Healthy ears (*bottom, left*) should be clean, free from any discharge and have no sign of unpleasant odor. A waxy discharge or an apparent irritation are signs of an ear infection.

X-rays have greatly simplified the diagnosis and treatment of limb fractures. They help in ascertaining the most suitable means of fixation of a broken limb and in checking progress towards healing (*right*).

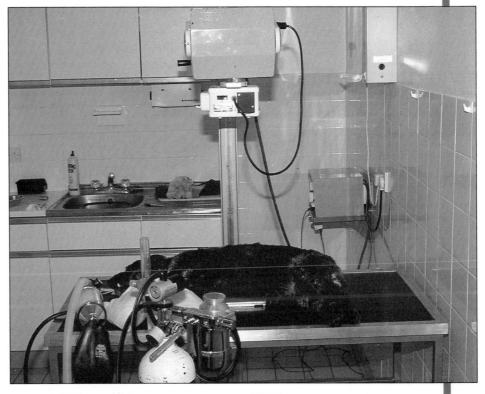

act as specialists in specific areas. It may even be possible to reduce costs, for a more efficient practice. Nevertheless, this does mean that you may not be able to see the same veterinarian on every visit. This is not crucial, however, because your dog's records will be on the premises and can be used by any member of the team.

This does not apply if you go from practice to practice. To change without notifying your existing veterinarian appears off-hand, and it also means that the dog's previous medical history and laboratory test results will not be available to the new veterinarian. This can make his or her work more difficult, and can be dangerous for your dog and more expensive for you if tests have to be repeated. If you are unhappy with treatment you have received, you can transfer to another veterinary practice without any problem. The only proviso is that you notify the original practice beforehand; long, detailed explanations will not be required. Simply telephone and say you are changing to another veterinarian, or write if you prefer. This will also be necessary if you move out of the area, but your new veterinarian can refer back to previous treatment.

? IS IT POSSIBLE FOR MY VETERINARIAN TO GIVE ME ADVICE OVER THE TELEPHONE?

Most veterinary practices are busy and receive a large number of calls during the day. Some are likely to be emergencies. It is very difficult for a veterinarian to get a clear picture of a case without actually seeing the patient for an examination. You should, therefore, be prepared to take your dog to the office initially. Once treatment has begun, however, telephone for advice if you are concerned, but keep your call as brief as possible. Some unscrupulous clients will use the telephone in the hope of obtaining free service; in some veterinary practices, a charge is made for telephone advice depending on the circumstances. Do not expect to be able to speak to your veterinarian automatically, especially if you have not called at a pre-arranged time. During the course of the day, the veterinarian may be tied up in a consultation or operating when you telephone. His staff will be able to deal with your query, referring to the veterinarian when this is necessary and as soon as possible.

? WILL MY VETERINARIAN VISIT MY DOG AT HOME?

This depends on individual circumstances. As a general rule, you should take your dog to the veterinarian's office where specialist help and equipment such as an X-ray machine are available. This will also be less expensive. Home visits are extremely time-consuming, and the cost has to be passed on to the client. A veterinarian may call in an emergency situation, however, such as when a bitch encounters difficulties while giving birth. Most dogs tend to be easier to handle out of their own territory and this is another reason for taking your dog to the vet's office if possible.

? MY DOG SEEMS FINE, BUT I AM WONDERING IF HE SHOULD BE CHECKED REGULARLY BY THE VETERINARIAN?

Providing your dog appears healthy, there is probably little point in visiting your veterinarian. But be sure deworming and inoculations are kept up to date. This will probably involve a visit once or twice a year and your veterinarian can examine your dog then to check its state of health.

GENERAL NURSING

An owner can do much to assist the recovery of a dog if it becomes ill, or is injured in a domestic or road accident, although in the first instance, veterinary advice is likely to be required without delay.

? MY DOG HAS TO BE ANESTHETIZED, AND I HAVE TO LEAVE IT WITH THE VETERINARIAN OVERNIGHT. IS THIS ROUTINE?

Yes, as a general rule, but it depends on individual circumstances. You will probably be asked to see that your dog receives nothing to eat or drink for a period beforehand. Under the effects of the anesthetic, vomiting can occur and food or fluid can pass down into the lungs. Since the dog will not be able to cough as normal, this could have fatal consequences. A full stomach may also interfere with breathing when the dog is unconscious. If you suspect that your dog has scavenged something during the critical period beforehand, notify your veterinarian right away. It may be possible for him to attend to another patient and reschedule your dog's operation if necessary.

The risk of administering an anesthetic to a dog is normally low. If the veterinarian is especially concerned, he will discuss the relevant factors with you. Obviously, old, obese dogs face a higher risk than young, healthy dogs. Complications are more likely to arise with certain breeds. In the case of the Greyhound, for example, there is little body fat to absorb the barbiturate anesthetic administered by injection. If this is used, the dose will have to be adjusted accordingly. Such factors can also influence the recovery time. It is quite usual for a veterinarian to keep the dog under close supervision until it has recovered from the immediate effects of the anesthetic as well as the operation, for your dog's sake.

GIVING A PILL

First hold your dog's muzzle with one hand and tilt her nose up a little; put your thumb in the space between the canine tooth and the first molar and press it against the roof of the mouth — this will force the dog to keep its mouth open. With your other hand, drop the medication as far back in the dog's mouth as you can, make sure the pill is on top of the tongue, not under it. Then hold the mouth closed and gently massage the throat until you feel the dog swallow the pill. It may help to persuade your dog to swallow a pill by camouflaging it with a favorite snack.

? MY VETERINARIAN PRESCRIBED A COURSE OF PILLS. HOW SHOULD I GIVE THESE TO MY DOG?

The simplest method is to disguise the pills in food, as long as they do not have to be given at a separate time from meals. The best way is to conceal the pill in a suitable piece of meat because dogs can readily detect the presence of an inedible object in their food. If you have more than one dog, make sure the correct dog consumes the pills and actually swallows them.

It may be necessary in some cases to administer the pill directly. This is not difficult with a dog that is used to being handled, but it can prove difficult in other cases. The key to success is to place the pill at the very back of the mouth so that the dog will swallow it almost automatically rather than attempting to spit it out. Grasp the upper jaw on either side with one hand, and raise, holding the lower jaw with the other hand and using your first finger and thumb to pop the pill onto the base of the tongue. Hold the mouth closed, keeping the head slightly raised and tickling the throat so as to encourage the dog to swallow. For a right-handed person, the pill should be inserted with this hand. If you dislike placing your hand in the dog's mouth, use a pair of forceps for the purpose. There are also automatic dispensers that can be used. Try to give the pill on the first attempt. The dog is likely to become increasingly restless if the process proves protracted.

? HOW SHOULD I ADMINISTER LIQUID MEDICINE TO MY DOG?

Probably the easiest means of giving liquid to a dog is with a syringe. The required quantity can be measured precisely, and then the syringe can be placed at the back of the dog's mouth from the right side, and its contents emptied with steady pressure from the right hand. The left hand is used to open the mouth sufficiently to allow the syringe to be placed within the dog's mouth while restraining both jaws. The situation is reversed for a left-handed

GIVING MEDICINE

First, measure the precise amount of medication into a syringe. Hold your dog's snout and place the syringe at the back of the dog's mouth, from the right side, in the gap between the canine teeth and molars. Empty the contents of the syringe with steady pressure using your right hand. The left hand can be used to open the dog's mouth sufficiently to allow the syringe to be slipped into place and also to restrain the jaws. If the dog chokes, let the head down without relinquishing your grip. Do not tilt the head too far back — this will lead to coughing as fluid enters the larynx.

HOW CRITICAL ARE THE DOSAGE DIRECTIONS THAT MY VETERINARIAN HAS GIVEN FOR MY DOG'S MEDICINE?

You should always try to follow directions as closely as possible. Certainly, if the directions say to administer medicine before a meal, this is important. Some drugs, such as tetracyclines, are not absorbed well from the intestinal tract in the presence of food; calcium combines with this group of antibiotics leaving lower quantities to be absorbed. Its effectiveness in fighting infection is correspondingly reduced. With regard to times of dosage, it is also important to adhere to these as far as possible. This will insure that a therapeutically active level of the drug is retained within the body at all times during the course of treatment. The required dose will be specified by your veterinarian and will vary according to the size and weight of your dog. If the pills need to be given twice daily, give them at, say, 8.00 am in the morning, and at the same time at night. The precise time is not as important as the time interval during which the level of the drug in the body is declining. It does no good to give the dog one or two pills then stop. In order to be effective, they must be administered regularly for at least five days. In certain circumstances, as with eye infections where the tear fluid is constantly washing the medication away, more treatment will be needed during the course of a day.

HOW CAN I KEEP MY DOG WARM? ARE THERE ANY DANGERS ATTACHED TO USING A HOT WATER BOTTLE IN HIS BASKET?

The methods suggested earlier (on p.95) for young puppies are all applicable for a sick dog. An infra-red heater placed out of the dog's reach above the sleeping area is probably most satisfactory, providing that there is also a cooler spot accessible to the dog. A heating pad can be used in the basket, and a hot water bottle is also suitable, as long as you make sure that the dog cannot burn itself accidentally. This applies especially in the case of a dog which is in a semi-comatose state and unable to move easily. The most important factor is to use warm water only, as boiling water can burn the skin. Wrap the hot water bottle in a thick towel as an additional precaution. Rubber bottles are

person. In both cases, it is helpful to have someone else available to restrain the dog for you. If you run the medicine in slowly, the dog should not attempt to choke. If it does, let the head down without relinquishing your grip. The head needs to be positioned at an angle of about 45° from the horizontal. Do not tilt it too far back as this will lead to coughing as fluid enters the larynx.

It is much harder to administer liquid medicine to a dog by means of a spoon, especially if you must give a specific amount. Avoid filling a spoon full because it will spill much more easily. Dosing will be easier to carry out if the dog is at a reasonable height off the ground — stand it on a table, for example, but protect the surface, both from the dog's claws and any spilled medicine.

Afterwards, wash the syringe or spoon thoroughly. Do not forget to show affection to the dog and give it a tidbit if it has been well-behaved. It is a useful idea to open a puppy's mouth regularly, so that in later life, it will let you administer treatments via the mouth when required.

The medication may have a sugar or similar coating; it is vital that you do not break pills of this type because they may then have an extremely bitter and unpleasant taste and may also cause the dog to salivate profusely. The dog will probably resent any future attempts to give it pills. If you need help to restrain the dog, get someone else to restrain the neck with an arm so that the dog cannot slip away from you.

Initial dosing may lead to a noticeable improvement in the dog's condition, and it may appear as healthy as ever before the course of pills is completed. Nevertheless, always be sure to give all the pills prescribed by your veterinarian following the directions on the packaging, implicitly. Failure to give a full course of antibiotics may not only cause the condition to reappear but can also lead to bacterial resistance to further treatment by the drug concerned. Antibiotics have altered the face of veterinary medicine, but they are not of value in every instance.

preferable to those of stone which are uncomfortable for the dog to lie on, and make sure the top is fitted properly and that the rubber is in good condition because otherwise water will saturate the dog's bed rapidly.

? HOW CAN I FIND MY DOG'S HEARTBEAT IN AN EMERGENCY?

Flex the elbow joint on the left-side of the body to its maximum extent. This will give you the approximate position of the heart. It should be possible to feel the heartbeat, particularly after exercise as long as the dog is not excessively overweight.

? WHAT CARE DOES A PARAPLEGIC DOG REQUIRE?

A dog which is unable to walk (usually because of spinal injury) needs considerable care. If it lies in the same position over a long period, it may develop pressure sores, particularly on bony parts of the body. Bigger, heavier dogs run the greatest risk. Pressure sores should not be confused with the thickening skin commonly seen on the elbows of healthy dogs of the large breeds although the case is similar. These come from lying on hard surfaces for any length of time.

Caring for a paraplegic dog is a considerable undertaking. It can be made easier by making a foam bed with removable covers, or by encouraging the dog to lie on a bean-bag. Do not allow the dog to remain in the same position for more than a couple of hours, and if any

The position of the heart is most easily found by flexing the elbow joint against the body on the left-hand side. The tip of the joint provides the approximate position where the heartbeat can be detected, using a finger gently applied between the ribs. In this case (*right*) a veterinarian is using a stethoscope to amplify the heartbeat.

TAKING A DOG'S PULSE

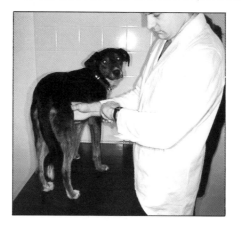

There are various places on a dog's body to take its pulse, but the femoral artery, running down each hind limb is probably the easiest site. Do not press too hard when taking a pulse, or the sensation will be dulled.

sores appear and form ulcers, contact your veterinarian. An additional problem is that such dogs are likely to be incontinent so their surroundings must be easy to clean thoroughly.

? WILL I EVER HAVE TO GIVE MY DOG AN INJECTION? NEEDLES WORRY ME!

The only circumstance in which you are likely to have to administer injections to your dog is if it becomes diabetic. Your veterinarian will show you how to carry out the necessary injections of insulin, and if you are concerned, you can practice

using an orange as a substitute for the skin. The insulin will have to be administered subcutaneously (under the skin rather than into a vein, which makes the process easier). Having filled the syringe, scruff the loose skin on the back of the dog's neck and insert the needle through the skin. Draw back slightly to insure that no blood appears in the syringe (this would indicate that you had struck a blood vessel) and if all is well, push the plunger firmly and then withdraw the needle. It is important to use a new needle each time, not only on grounds of hygiene but also because they blunt rapidly. Dog's skin is surprisingly

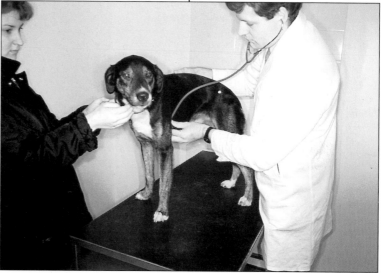

A sudden stroke may well be indicated by a slight and subtle tilt of your dog's head, with the tongue possibly hanging out (*below*). This is a serious condition and you should contact your vet immediately in this instance.

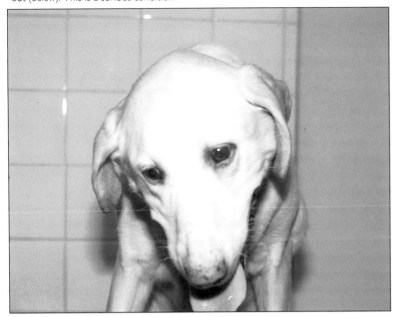

TAKING A TEMPERATURE

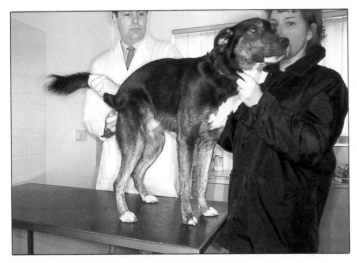

Raise the tail with the left hand and insert the thermometer — which should be lubricated with petroleum jelly — with the other hand, into the anus. The thermometer should be held in place for about three minutes. Take care to restrain the dog while doing this. Normal temperature is about 101.5°F, but a slight rise after exercise is normal.

tough, and a blunt needle makes the process more difficult. Dispose of your old needles carefully by placing the protective covers back on them and returning them to your veterinarian. These injections will probably have to be administered on a daily basis.

? IS IT TRUE THAT A DOG'S NOSE WILL FEEL WET IF IT IS HEALTHY?

This is generally accepted as a sign of good health; the moisture is produced largely in the lateral nasal glands in the nose. But dogs that are dehydrated but otherwise healthy will have dry noses because the body responds by reducing fluid output via urine and even in the nasal glands. A dog that has been sitting in a warm spot may also have a temporarily dry nose. In addition, a dog that has recovered from distemper at an early age may be left with a nose that is permanently dry.

? WHAT CONSTITUTES AN EMERGENCY SITUATION IN WHICH I SHOULD CONTACT MY VETERINARIAN WITHOUT DELAY?

Conditions which require rapid veterinary attention are normally those of sudden onset. If your dog collapses, appears unable to breathe, lose conciousness or starts having convulsions, then you must contact your veterinarian without delay. Injuries from accidents can also be life-threatening. In addition to giving first-aid on the spot, you should contact a veterinarian at once. Serious hemorrhaging, obvious fracture, poisoning, drowning or scalding are cases in point. Also, any problems during whelping are likely to require urgent veterinary attention.

? HOW DO I KNOW WHEN TO CONTACT MY VETERINARIAN?

If you are concerned, seek professional advice without delay. Some cases are less urgent than others, however, and if you do not feel that it is an emergency, arrange an appointment at a convenient time. A veterinarian will always see a genuine emergency at any time of the day or night but will not welcome being called out in a case where the dog has been ill for two weeks and you have chosen to do nothing until late on a Sunday night.

INFECTIOUS DISEASES

The majority of these are positively life-threatening, yet the threat can be overcome successfully by means of preventative inoculations. All dogs should be protected against these killer diseases.

? IS DISTEMPER THE SAME DISEASE AS HARD PAD?

Hard pad is a form of distemper, in which a virus attacks the outer layer of the skin of the foot pads and nose, causing callus-like pads to form on the feet and thick horny-like skin to form on the nose. The disease is caused by a virus, and aside from its immediate effects, distemper can lead to serious long-term complications. It is spread by close contact between dogs, often from urine, and first invades the tonsils and neighboring lymph nodes. In some cases, antibodies are produced by the dog's defense system at this stage, and they overcome the infection. In these cases, the dog feels ill but recovers uneventfully.

If antibodies are not produced, the virus invades the body and becomes widely disseminated, usually about three weeks later. A variety of symptoms ranging from a high temperature to diarrhea and vomiting will appear. More specific effects on the nervous system will also appear in over 50 percent of such cases. But these may not develop until years later; in the meantime the virus remains within the spinal cord and brain. Under stress, serious neurological signs ranging from fits to paralysis will appear, and twitching of the facial muscles is often seen. While this can be controlled, other symptoms may not respond to treatment, and the dog may have to be put to sleep on humanitarian grounds.

It may be possible to recognize a dog in later life that was afflicted with distemper as a puppy by examining its teeth. The virus causes the surface layer to take on a rough brownish appearance if the enamel had not been fully developed at the time of the infection. Other signs are a dry, cracked nose and the thickened foot pads in some cases. The symptoms of distemper are variable in severity, but any dog suffering from a generalized infection will appear seriously ill.

? IS IT POSSIBLE TO PROTECT AGAINST DISTEMPER? IS IT TRUE THAT HUMAN MEASLES VACCINE CAN BE OF USE FOR THIS PURPOSE?

Every owner should have his dog inoculated against this highly unpleasant disease. However, many forget or simply do not bother until an epidemic occurs. The infection can be spread by wild canids including foxes, raccoons, badgers and ferrets. Young dogs run a particular risk since, without inoculation, they possess no immunity to the disease from about 12 weeks of age on. It is important to maintain inoculation cover because older dogs can succumb, especially if they have spent much of their lives in an area where there were few dogs and they were unlikely to encounter the virus. An inoculated dog in an urban area is almost certain to be exposed to the infection (which has a worldwide incidence) but, being protected, will not develop clinical signs. A subsequent challenge boosts the antibody level still further and improves the dog's immunity.

The distemper virus belongs to the same group as the measles virus, but the disease cannot be spread to humans. Nevertheless, measles vaccine can indeed protect young puppies against distemper in a specific situation where the traditional distemper vaccine would be ineffective. Dogs less than eight weeks old cannot be inoculated against distemper because the antibodies in the mother's milk will overcome the vaccine.

Measles vaccine is unaffected by maternal antibodies. It can be used to build up the puppy's immune system to give it early protection in a situation where it could be at grave risk. For example, measles vaccine might be used in a welfare kennel where a bitch whose history is unknown gives birth at a time when there is a distemper outbreak among other dogs in the same environment. Should you feel that puppies need measles vaccine, refer to your veterinarian, not your doctor.

? IS IT TRUE THAT THERE ARE TWO DIFFERENT FORMS OF CANINE ADENOVIRUS WHICH HAVE WIDELY DIFFERING EFFECTS?

Yes. Canine adenovirus type 1, abbreviated to CAV-1 results in infectious canine hepatitis (ICH), also known as Rubarth's Disease. The route of transmission is highly significant. When taken into the body via the mouth, its effects will be on the liver. If inhaled, a less

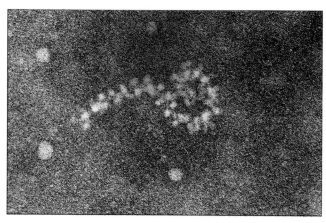

Coronavirus in dogs is a relatively new disease, first recognized in 1978 in show dogs in the United States.

Fortunately, a vaccine has already been developed to offer protection against this unpleasant, contagious disease.

TRANSMISSION OF A VIRUS

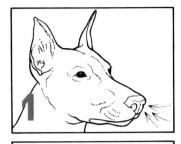
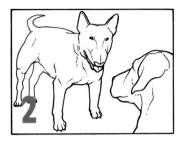

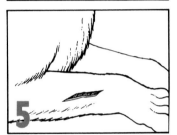

Diseases are more likely to spread where there is a high density of dogs, for example, at a show or in boarding kennels. Kennel cough is spread by airborne viruses (**1**). Some of the more resistant viruses may either simply be transmitted directly on contact (**2**) or, from contaminated items such as bedding, grooming implements and feeding bowls. Scavenging dogs are susceptible to disease by ingesting contaminated foods (**3**). Other kinds of virus can be spread by animal vectors — bites from insects such as ticks or, in the case of rabies, bites from other mammals (**4**). Open cuts or wounds are another danger as viruses are often carried in the bloodstream (**5**). A particular danger to developing puppies is that some viruses are small enough to pass across the placenta or contaminate the mother's milk and so infect puppies either before or soon after they are born (**6**).

severe disease affecting the respiratory tract is likely to occur. Some dogs overcome the infection in the early stages and few clinical symptoms appear. Young dogs again run the greatest risk of infection.

The typical symptoms of hepatitis resulting from an inflamed liver will appear. Characteristically, these include jaundice in which the inside of the mouth and other mucous membranes take on a yellowish hue. The lymph nodes throughout the body become swollen. Hemorrhages may occur because the blood clotting system is also affected by the virus. Infected dogs may die suddenly without necessarily appearing very ill beforehand. Those that do recover may be afflicted with "blue eye," a bluish opacity that covers one or both eyes for a brief period. The dog's appetite will return. The virus itself is likely to localize in the kidneys and be excreted in the urine for a

considerable period of time during which it can be transmitted to other dogs. The weight loss that occurred during the acute stage of the disease will be resolved slowly. There is evidence to suggest that infection with CAV-1 can create permanent kidney damage, and that it may be a contributory cause of chronic renal failure in old age.

Prevention is straightforward and entails inoculation early in life with annual boosters. There is a slight danger that live vaccine may give rise to blue eye — Afghan Hounds are most susceptible to this symptom. By way of contrast, the second form of adenovirus, CAV-2, tends to localize in the respiratory tract and is one of the causes of *kennel cough*. A vaccine is also available to protect against this form of adenovirus. Kennel cough is normally mild but can lead to pneumonia if it goes untreated; it is a disease that is contagious and spreads as fast as 'flu. However it can be treated by antibiotics.

? WE ARE GOING TO STAY ON A FARM FOR A FEW DAYS. WILL OUR DOG BE AT RISK FROM LEPTOSPIROSIS?

Two forms of this bacterial disease are recognized; they are caused by *Leptospira icterohaemorrhagiae* and *Leptospira canicola*. The former serotype is linked with rats, and dogs such as terriers can run a risk in agricultural areas where they come into contact with the bacterium via urine. A dog on the farm that has recovered could also be a source of infection as it too will be excreting the bacteria in its urine. Infection with *Leptospira icterohaemorrhagiae* usually leads to jaundice; early symptoms are also likely to include diarrhea, vomiting and a fever. Antibiotics are of value in combating this disease. In the latter stages, the body temperature falls significantly, and the dog may experience difficulty in breathing and drink at every opportunity.

Regular inoculations will protect your dog against many of the serious or fatal infectious diseases.
Vaccinations against rabies is compulsory in many states. Today, vaccines can be given together in a single "cocktail' and are administered subcutaneously (*right*), as painlessly as possible.

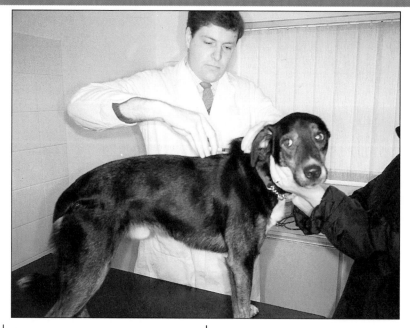

? PARVOVIRUS INFECTION OF DOGS RECEIVED WIDESPREAD PUBLICITY SEVERAL YEARS AGO. IS IT STILL A THREAT?

Yes, but inoculation has helped reduce the incidence of this disease. It first appeared during the late 1970s, and soon spread worldwide. The reasons for its onset are not fully understood yet. It may well have been a mutant form of the *feline panleukopenia virus* which is also a *parvovirus*, "parvo" means small and refers to the size of the individual virus particles. Two distinct effects of parvovirus in dogs are now well-recognized. In the case of puppies under five weeks of age, the virus affects the heart muscle and leads to sudden death from heart failure. Some puppies may survive, but they have a poor prognosis because the damage to their heart is irreversible; they can die suddenly and unexpectedly at a later time from the affects of the earlier *myocarditis* (inflammation of the heart muscle).

Older dogs usually develop the typical blood-stained diarrhea as the virus attacks the intestinal lining. They may also vomit, and dehydration rapidly follows. Treatment is likely to necessitate the use of an intravenous drip, and a full recovery cannot be guaranteed. There is a good chance of permanent damage to the gut, and this in turn can restrict the absorption of foodstuffs. The weight loss is almost impossible to overcome after the acute stage of the illness has passed. In addition,

intermittent outbreaks of diarrhea are likely to occur throughout the remainder of the dog's life. The recommended inoculation procedure depends to some extent on the breed concerned in the case of puppies. Check with your veterinarian. Parvovirus in dogs is a serious illness, and it makes sense to have your dog protected.

The virus itself is very durable and can exist outside the body for at least a year. It is also resistant to many disinfectants. It can be spread by clothes and shoes as well as through more obvious routes such as feeding bowls. After an outbreak, the premises should be washed thoroughly with sodium hypochlorite (bleach). Protective footwear which can be immersed in a solution of bleach should be worn to minimize the risk of spreading the disease to uninoculated dogs.

? DOES INOCULATION PROVIDE AN ABSOLUTE GUARANTEE THAT MY DOG WILL BE SAFE FROM SERIOUS DISEASES SUCH AS PARVOVIRUS?

Unfortunately, there is no such guarantee, but if the vaccine is correctly administered, it should, apart from a few exceptional cases, provide full protection against the diseases concerned. To work, a vaccine must activate the body's immune system. If this does not happen (if maternal antibodies neutralize the vaccine in a young puppy, for example), then there will be little or no protection later in life. This

is why inoculations are repeated in a young dog (see p.33). The immune system in a tiny minority of dogs may be unable to respond after the influence of maternal antibodies wears off. It is possible to measure the antibody response to a vaccine, but this is not carried out routinely because it tends to be expensive, and vaccines are usually extremely efficient. There is certainly no valid reason for not having a dog inoculated on the grounds that the vaccine will be ineffective.

Manufacturers are spending vast sums of money on research and development of vaccines for dogs and are constantly monitoring their effectiveness. It is known that certain drugs, notably *corticosteroids*, depress the body's immune response. Inoculations when the dog is receiving such treatments are not to be recommended. Similarly, if your bitch is pregnant, she must not receive a live vaccine because this could harm the developing puppies. As a dog gets older, it is less able to produce antibodies, and regular inoculations thus assume increasing importance towards the end of a dog's life.

? HOW SAFE ARE VACCINES?

The likelihood of adverse reactions occurring is extremely small, and symptoms are likely to appear within minutes of the vaccine's administration. The symptoms can normally be reversed by an injection of adrenalin. There is virtually no risk of your dog developing the disease when it is given a live vaccine. If it does succumb to distemper within a few days, for example, this is likely to be due to the fact that it was already incubating the disease before it was inoculated. In other words, the vaccine could not evoke its normal protective response because the infection was already present in the body.

 IS IT POSSIBLE TO INOCULATE ORPHANED PUPPIES?

These run a great risk if they have not received any protective colostrum, especially in kennel surroundings where other dogs are present. In these cases, it is preferable to give a *hyperimmune serum* because the puppy's own immune system cannot manufacture antibodies from birth when challenged by the vaccine. The puppy can be vaccinated for the first time approximately one month after the administration of the serum.

 SHOULD MY DOG BY INOCULATED AGAINST RABIES?

Rabies or hydrophobia (fear of water) is one of the most dangerous viral infections, fatal to unimmunized dogs. Because this disease is also dangerous to humans, any suspicion of rabies must be reported to public health authorities. If you or your dog have come into contact with a dog suspected of being rabid, your dog must be quarantined and you must submit to complete medical treatment. Immunization can protect your dog from this fatal disease.

 HOW DOES RABIES SPREAD?

In North America, before 1951, all cases of human rabies were caused by either cat or dog bites. But, following extensive vaccination campaigns, dog-borne rabies has been virtually unknown in the United States since 1951. However, a growing number of wild animals such as foxes, rabbits, bats, skunks and raccoons have been reported as carriers in the United States and it is unlikely that the disease will ever be totally eliminated.

HOW WOULD I KNOW IF MY DOG HAD RABIES? WHAT EMERGENCY ACTION SHOULD I TAKE IF I AM BITTEN?

The onset of clinical symptoms of rabies can take several weeks or months. In the early stages of rabies, the dog will be moody — irritable at one moment, then affectionate. It is hypersensitive to noise and light. It eats stones and pieces of wood and other indigestible objects while refusing normal food. Later stages are marked by running amok, attacking and biting, difficulties in swallowing, and excessive drooling.

You do not have to be bitten to succumb to rabies. The virus can be transmitted in the saliva just before clinical symptoms appear. This is clearly the most dangerous period for the owner. Any cuts on the hand, if contaminated with saliva, can provide access to the body for the virus. If you have the misfortune to be bitten by a dog that could have rabies, wash the cut immediately using alcohol, if available, or rinse under running water and treat the wound with iodine. Contact your doctor without delay so that appropriate medical treatment can be arranged immediately. This should ensure that the disease does not develop; once symptoms are apparent, the likelihood of recovery is virtually zero. In areas where the disease is endemic, supervise children closely, especially if

IMMUNITY TO DISEASE

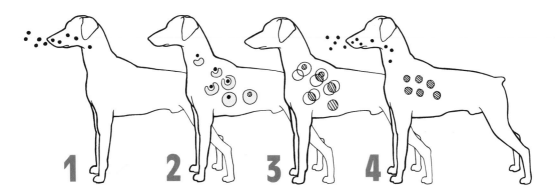

When foreign organisms such as bacteria or viruses enter the body, they stimulate the host to produce antibodies that attach to the organisms and neutralize them (**1**). These antibodies are produced both at the site of entry — the nose or intestines — and in the bloodstream by white blood cells, the lymphocytes (**2**). Once neutralized the organisms can be engulfed by other white cells in the blood, the macrophages, and broken down (**3**). A vaccine stimulates the body to produce antibodies so that it can respond more quickly to future infection (**4**).

ANIMAL VECTORS OF RABIES

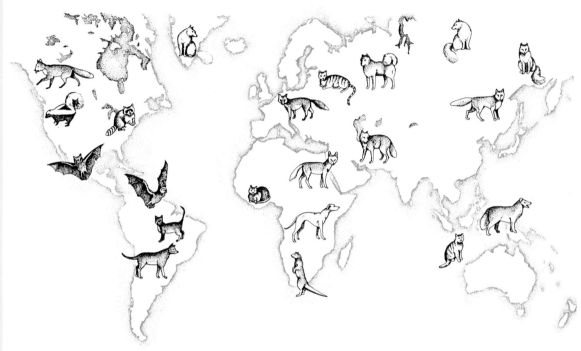

The distribution of rabies is world-wide and in places where the disease occurs regularly there is usually a "reservoir" of the infection in wild animals — foxes in Western Europe, skunks and racoons in the United States, mongooses in South Africa, India and the Caribbean and vampire bats in Central and South America. Australia, the United Kingdom, Antarctica and Hawaii are the few rabies-free places in the world — thanks to their isolation by water and extremely strict import controls.

they are unfamiliar with this disease. Some wild animals suffering from rabies can appear friendly and are thus extremely dangerous. Although the symptoms of the disease are most fearsome in carnivores, rabies is equally lethal for herbivores such as cattle. The major source of infection for humans, however, is dog bites.

 IS THERE ANY OTHER DISEASE THAT COULD BE CONFUSED WITH RABIES?

It is possible that *Aujeszky's Disease*, a viral disease usually associated with pigs, can produce similar symptoms; it is called pseudo-rabies. Dogs living on pig farms or those which have gained access to contaminated uncooked pork run the greatest risk of infection. Affected dogs will paw and scratch their faces and show no signs of aggression. An initial phase of excitement leads to other neurological symptoms and finally to a coma about two weeks after infection. No treatment is available. The disease presents no threat to human health.

CAN MY DOG GET KENNEL COUGH IN THE HOME?

It is possible but less likely than at kennels or shows where large numbers of dogs congregate, especially if air space is limited and ventilation poor. There is no single organism responsible for *kennel cough*, or *infectious tracheobronchitis* as it is also known. The bacterium *Bordetella bronchoseptica* can be isolated in the majority of cases, however, and it leads to a cough which can become severe. The cough occurs whenever the throat region over the trachea is touched. The nose is also likely to be affected — a thick nasal discharge is frequently seen. In addition to the bacterial involvement, viruses may also be implicated, notably canine adenovirus type 2 (CAV-2). CAV-1 may also give rise to the condition if the viral particles are inhaled. *Canine parainfluenza virus* is sometimes involved as well as other *pathogens* such as *mycoplasmas*, but these are less significant.

In any event, kennel cough tends to be self-limiting and is not often a life-threatening disease although it is very unpleasant for the dog. Complications such as pneumonia are likely to arise in the older dog. The symptoms should routinely disappear within about three weeks, but recurrent cases in kenneled dogs are not unusual because immunity tends to be transient. In any event, an effective vaccine against all the main causes of kennel cough is now available, and its use is to be recommended in dogs that are being kenneled or attending shows regularly. This vaccine may be given intra-nasally (sprayed up the nostrils) in some cases rather than being injected as it usually is with young puppies.

PROBLEMS DOWN BELOW

Incontinence is disturbing for the dog as well as the owner, since dogs do appreciate that they should not soil carpets in the home. Bitches are often more prone to urinary problems of this type, after spaying.

? WHAT ARE THE CAUSES OF DIARRHEA? HOW SERIOUS IS IT?

Diarrhea is not a disease but a symptom associated with various conditions, some of which are infectious. Bacterial diseases, such as *salmonellosis*, and viruses mentioned previously can all cause diarrhea. Parasites, such as *Coccidia*, which is a unicellular organism described as a *protozoa*, may also be implicated in some cases. Non-infectious causes include malabsorption of certain foodstuffs, which may be caused, for example, by pancreatic insufficiency.

In any given case, veterinary advice may be needed, but this is especially true when puppies are affected because they can rapidly become dehydrated. In an older dog, withholding food for 24 hours and then offering a small bland meal of chicken and rice, for example, can resolve the problem assuming the dog appears healthy otherwise. Diarrhea can result from scavenging unsuitable or old food.

Any trace of fresh blood in your dog's stools suggests that there is a digestive disorder in the lower part of the digestive tract. Inflammation of the large bowel, known as *colitis*, is a typical condition which causes such symptoms. The feces are almost jelly-like in appearance because of their high mucous content. If the source of the blood loss is the small intestine, there will be no fresh blood in the feces because the blood will have been partially digested as it moved through the gut and will have taken on a reddish-brown appearance.

? WHAT ARE THE ANAL GLANDS? MY VETERINARIAN SAYS THAT MY DOG HAS BLOCKED ANAL SACS WHICH NEED EMPTYING.

The anal glands are really sacs which produce a secretion that is deposited on the feces and can be recognized by other dogs. The first sign of a blockage is likely to be the dog rubbing its rear quarters along the ground in a bid to overcome the irritation. Such behavior is sometimes described as "scooting." The anal area becomes very tender and causes the dog considerable discomfort. It may try to bite itself. It is important to get the sacs emptied before defecation proves painful, and the area becomes infected. In severe cases, open channels *(fistulae)*, may develop around the anal ring. These can be difficult to heal successfully and may require cryosurgery.

Your veterinarian may be able to empty the sacs manually, but in more severe cases, the dog will have to be anesthetized. It will then be possible to wash the sacs out, and hopefully prevent a recurrence. Actual removal of the sacs may be necessary in chronic cases, but try adding bran to the dog's food, as this improves the roughage level of the diet and can help to resolve the problem. Most dogs have outlived the use of these glands.

? IS IT TRUE THAT BITCHES ARE MORE PRONE TO URINARY INFECTIONS THAN MALE DOGS?

Yes, because their urethras are shorter than those of male dogs. Ascending infections result in *cystitis*, inflammation of the bladder. Cystitis causes frequent urination and requires antibiotic treatment. In turn, an infection can be a predisposing factor in the development of bladder stones, known technically as *calculi*. The symptoms will depend on the part of the tract where the blockage has occurred. Difficulty in urinating will certainly be present, as will pain. It will probably be necessary for the veterinarian to examine the dog using a special contrast media X-ray technique to find the site of the problem. There are various options for treatment available, depending on the individual case. Some calculi may be washed through the tract or dislodged by means of a cannula, but recurrences in susceptible individuals are relatively common. A course of antibiotics may help to cure an underlying infection, but there can be a genetic susceptibility to urinary calculi as in the case of the Dalmatian because of metabolic defects. Other breeds prone to calculi are the Dachshunds and Corgis. Basset hounds can suffer.

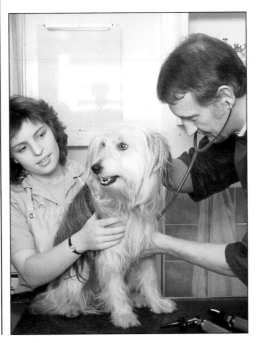

Stones in the urethra, kidneys or bladder give rise to difficulty in passing urine and the only option is to take your dog to the veterinarian (*left*) and have the stones removed surgically, under a general anesthetic.

EAR AND EYE PROBLEMS

Selective breeding has created some undesirable characteristics such as the heavy ears of Spaniels that are ideal sites for infections and hereditary eye disorders that may need surgical correction.

? WHAT ARE THE COMMON EYE DISORDERS IN DOGS?

The most significant inherited weakness is *progressive retinal atrophy* (PRA), a progressive deterioration of the cells of the retina at the back of the eye where the image impinges. Early symptoms will include poor night vision. The condition can be generalized extending over the whole retina or be confined to the central area as in Collies, Labradors and Briards. Dogs afflicted with generalized PRA include the various breeds of Poodle. Sadly, there is no treatment available. The characteristic changes can be seen, however, by using an ophthalmoscope to view the retina directly. If you suspect your dog is having difficulty in seeing, causing it to bump into objects around the home, consult your veterinarian.

Injury of the eye can result when a dog walks through undergrowth and a sharp twig or a similar object hits the eye. If there is any sign of blood, emergency treatment will be necessary. There are occasions when the surface of the eye is damaged causing a condition known as *keratitis*, which is usually painful. An ulcer can form at the site if the infection is left untreated, and this will be difficult to heal successfully. Breeds with relatively prominent eyes such as the Pekingese and the Pug are most likely to be affected.

? WHERE IS THE DOG'S THIRD EYELID? ARE EYELID PROBLEMS COMMON IN DOGS?

The third eyelid is rarely seen in a healthy dog. When the eye is closed, this fleshy membrane extends across the surface of

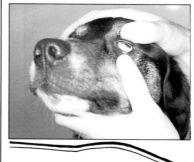

An ophthalmoscope enables a veterinarian to detect any eye problems early on (*above*), noting any changes in the retina at the rear of the eye which may herald the onset of the condition known as progressive retinal atrophy.

The third eyelid can be seen at the corner of the eye, nearest the nose (*left*). It should not be confused with the white sclera, which forms part of the eyeball itself.

ANATOMY OF A DOG'S EYE

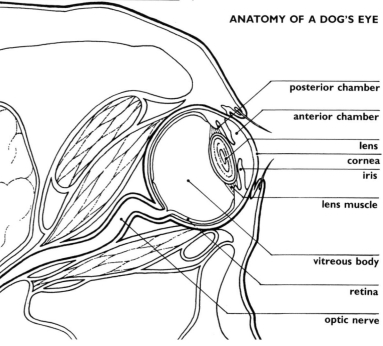

- posterior chamber
- anterior chamber
- lens
- cornea
- iris
- lens muscle
- vitreous body
- retina
- optic nerve

the eye beneath the external eyelids. If, however, the dog is sick and has lost weight, the fat behind the eyeball is reduced, and the eye sinks slightly in its socket revealing the third eyelid. It can be damaged and may even become inflamed. The incidence of eyelid disorders varies somewhat according to the breed of dog concerned. It is possible for the eyelids to be abnormally inverted so they rub on the surface of the eyeball and cause a condition known as *entropion*. This is relatively common in the St Bernard, Chow, Labrador and Golden Retriever as well as in various Setters. The reverse situation in which the lower eyelid is directed away from the eye is described as *ectropion* and often occurs in the Bloodhound and breeds of Spaniel. Surgical correction is required in many instances.

Another condition which may require surgery is the narrowing of tear ducts. This impairs drainage of fluid from the eye so the dog appears to be crying. It occurs in such breeds as the Poodle and Pekingese. The actual marks staining the face can be wiped away with cotton.

? ARE SOME DOGS MORE AT RISK FROM EAR INFECTIONS THAN OTHERS? WHAT IS THE LIKELIHOOD OF A CURE?

Any breed that has long floppy ears with a thick covering of hair is likely to be susceptible because the ear canal is occluded enabling bacteria and other potentially harmful micro-organisms to colonize the region. Regular, gentle cleaning of the ears can be particularly advantageous in dogs such as spaniels to help prevent infections of this type. Use a damp cotton swab for the purpose, taking care not to probe deeply within the ear but making sure the canal is free of dirt and wax.

A dog that scratches and rubs its ears repeatedly is likely to be suffering from an ear infection. There may also be an unpleasant odor associated with the ears. If the dog paws its ear repeatedly, it may injure the tissue on the earflap and cause blood to build up within, leading to a swelling called a *hematoma*. It may be necessary for a veterinarian to correct the hematoma by surgical means.

The major problem in curing ear infections is that the cause is not straightforward. Bacteria, fungi and sometimes ear mites can all be involved, and frequent use of medication tends to lead to antibiotic resistance. In addition, treatment usually needs to be maintained for a relatively long period of time to prevent recurrence. When there is no improvement, surgery will probaby be the only solution. In an operation called an *aural resection*, the vertical part of the ear canal is opened permanently. This will not be noticeable when the ear flap is in its usual position. If a dog suddenly appears to have great pain in its ear, the cause is likely to be a grass seed or a similar foreign body, not an infection. In most cases of this type veterinary advice should be sought.

? HOW SHOULD I ADMINISTER EYE MEDICATION?

This usually comes in the form of drops or an ointment. Check that the dog's head is adequately restrained and then cautiously apply the fluid as close as possible to the eye without actually touching the surface. If necessary, pull the lids apart gently, bearing in mind that the dog will probably blink when the medication makes contact with the eye itself. Ointment is perhaps easier to apply since there is no risk of it being washed away with a blink, but restrain the dog for a few moments following application so that it does not wipe off the medication.

GIVING EYE DROPS

Hold your dog's head steady and carefully drop the medication into the eye; try to avoid splashing eye drops out of the eye as the dog blinks. Treatment may well need to be applied several times daily.

ANATOMY OF A DOG'S EAR

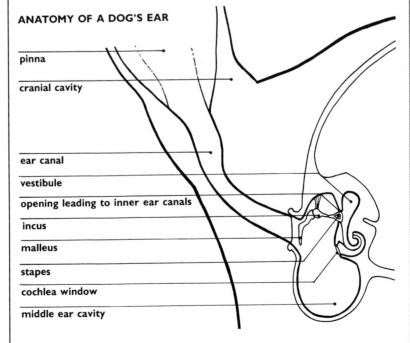

pinna

cranial cavity

ear canal

vestibule

opening leading to inner ear canals

incus

malleus

stapes

cochlea window

middle ear cavity

METABOLIC DISORDERS

These can sometimes be of acute onset, such as milk fever in a suckling bitch, although generally, these conditions tend to be more insidious and can be rather variable in their effects on the body.

? **MY DOG HAS BEEN LOSING WEIGHT OVER A PERIOD OF TIME WHILE MAINTAINING A HEALTHY APPETITE. MY VETERINARIAN HAS SUGGESTED IT COULD BE PANCREATIC INSUFFICIENCY. WHAT IS THIS, AND IS TREATMENT POSSIBLE?**

The pancreas is a vital organ, producing both hormones, such as insulin, and enzymes to help digest the food in the small intestine. In a case of pancreatic insufficiency, there is an inadequate output of enzymes, leading to an incomplete breakdown of food for absorption into the body. As a result, the food is excreted in a relatively undigested state in pale-colored, loose feces with a highly unpleasant odor. Since the dog is not obtaining adequate nourishment from its food, it loses weight over a period of time. Pancreatic insufficiency can be confirmed by laboratory tests.

Treatment consists of providing sufficient enzymes via the food itself, usually in the form of capsules or powders, to compensate for the deficiency. It may also help to add ox sweetbread (pancreas) to the diet, and some formulated rations are of particular value for dogs suffering from this complaint. Alternatively, increase the level of protein relative to that of carbohydrate and fat. Unfortunately, although supplementation can improve the digestive process, affected dogs may not put on a great deal of weight and remain thin. While is it not difficult to cope with a dog suffering from pancreatic insufficiency compared to one suffering from *diabetes mellitus*, many owners find the prospect depressing and have their dog put to sleep.

? **ARE THERE TWO DIFFERENT FORMS OF DIABETES RECOGNIZED IN THE DOG?**

Yes. The most common type is known as *diabetes mellitus*, or sugar diabetes. This condition results from a deficiency of the hormone insulin which is produced by the pancreas and stimulates cells to take up glucose present in the blood stream. In the case of diabetes mellitus, the sugar accumulates in the bloodstream and the cells are deprived of this vital nutrient. Once a critical level is reached, glucose passes into the urine giving it an unusually sweet and sickly smell, and increasing volumes are passed. Body tissues are broken down to meet the body's energy requirement, and this leads to weakness.

Cushing's syndrome is characterized by the dog losing hair evenly on both sides of the body, and gaining a pot-bellied appearance (*above*). It results from an abnormality in the adrenal glands, positioned close to the kidneys. Glandular disorders can have other widespread effects.

128

Diabetes mellitus usually affects middle-aged dogs and is much more likely to be found in bitches. Once diagnosed, regular injections of insulin on a daily basis will probably be required, and the dog's condition will have to be closely monitored through regular urine samples.

The urine is also significant in the case of *diabetes insipidus*. A shortage of the *anti-diuretic hormone* (ADH) leads to a greatly increased output of urine, because water normally reabsorbed during its passage through the kidney is lost. As a result, the dog has a prodigious thirst to compensate for the increased water loss. Diabetes insipidus is a relatively rare condition, much less commonly seen than chronic renal failure which can produce similar symptoms. It is likely to be caused by a brain tumor. A synthetic form of the hormone can be administered to alleviate symptoms even if the actual source of the complaint cannot be corrected. Diabetes is a disease that can only be controlled rather than cured. The main signs of the disease, are excessive water intake , obesity and sweet-scented breath.

 WHAT DISORDERS CAN ARISE FROM A MALFUNCTION OF THE ADRENAL CORTEX? WILL EFFECTS BE SEEN THROUGHOUT THE BODY?

The adrenal glands are located close to the kidneys. The outer zone of these glands, known as the *cortex*, produce two hormones. Although relatively small, the adrenal glands have widespread effects, and any disorder has far-reaching consequences. The two hormones of significance are *cortisol* and *aldosterone*. If the level of output is relatively low, the condition known as *Addison's Disease* results. This is more often seen in bitches than in male dogs, and the symptoms are particularly apparent after exercise. Vomiting and a loss of appetite result from a deficiency of cortisol, while a shortage of aldosterone leads to dehydration. It is possible, once the condition has been diagnosed, to provide synthetic replacements keeping the dog in good health. The reverse situation, an excessive production of these hormones, results in *Cushing's syndrome*. Characteristic changes include uneven loss of hair on either side of the body and a weakness of the abdominal muscles, leading to a pot-bellied appearance. Although this, again, is a serious condition, some degree of treatment may be possible.

 COULD MY DOG BE SUFFERING FROM A THYROID GLAND DISORDER? IT SEEMS VERY INACTIVE.

The thyroid glands are important in regulating overall body activity. If the output of hormones is depressed, the dog is likely to appear listless, but there are more likely causes of such behavior. Other more typical symptoms of thyroid disorder include weight gain, greasy skin and a noticeable aversion to cold surroundings. In this case, pills given regularly will lead to a distinct improvement. A shortage of iodine in the diet may also cause similar symptoms, and for this reason, some breeders use kelp (seaweed) powder as a general tonic. Basenjis appear to have an unusually high requirement for iodine.

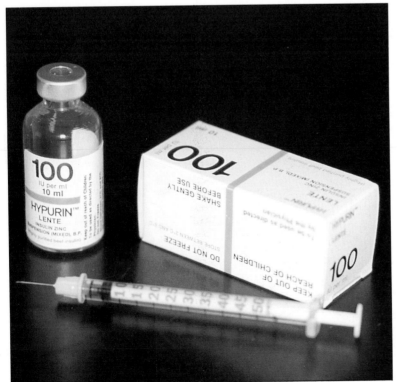

Diabetic dogs may show some similar symptoms to hyperthyroid dogs. Their urine should be tested regularly and a small dose of insulin (*left*) has to be injected by the owner each day. Insulin that has been produced for human diabetics is also used to treat dogs.

EXTERNAL PARASITES

While fleas are well-known, a range of other external parasites can also be encountered on dogs, some of which, such as Demodex mites can have very serious and infectious consequences.

? HOW WILL I KNOW IF MY DOG HAS FLEAS, AND HOW CAN I OVERCOME THIS PROBLEM?

Keep a close watch on the coat of your dog, especially during grooming. You may not immediately see fleas, but you are likely to spot their characteristic dark reddish-brown specks of dirt. These are the remains of the blood that fleas remove from their hosts. If placed on a piece of wet tissue or blotting paper, the dirt will tend to dissolve and create reddish rings. One of the major problems in combating fleas is that they spend relatively little time on their hosts but remain hidden in the environment for long periods. You might see a flea rushing through the hair of the dog around the base of the tail, a favored site on the body. Special flea combs are available, but such is the athleticism of fleas that even when detected, they are extremely difficult to catch. If you have an empty small container, fill it with water before you start grooming the dog (preferably outside) and keep it close at hand. Should a flea appear, it can be transferred to the water from which it should be unable to escape. Alternatively, squeeze it firmly between the thumb and index finger using your fingernail on its rear end to kill it.

The dog should be treated by means of a powder or an aerosol intended for this purpose. Be careful when applying these potentially toxic preparations; always read the directions carefully beforehand, especially if you buy one of the brands available through pet stores, because not all are safe for young dogs. With powder, brush it in against the natural lie of the

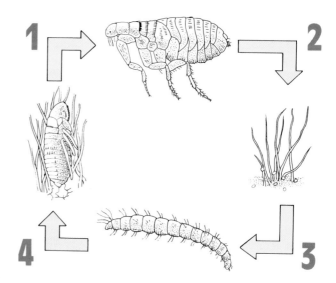

LIFE CYCLE OF A FLEA

The female dog flea (**1**) lays her eggs on the floor (**2**) or in bedding and in about a week they hatch into larvae (**3**) which spin cocoons, inside which the pupae (**4**) develop into adults within two or three weeks. The dog flea acts as an intermediate host for the larvae of the common tapeworm, *Dipylidium caninum* which makes it even more vital that flea infestations shoud be controlled. Also, dog fleas can bite the owner and in fact, the human flea, *Pulex irritans* often lives on dogs and vice versa.

coat. Use an aerosol in a similar manner taking particular care around the head to avoid the eyes. It is likely that the dog will attempt to lick some of the chemical out of its coat. To deter this, take your dog out for a walk immediately after applying the treatment. Do not be surprised if your dog is frightened by the noise of the aerosol. It is often preferable to opt for a powder for this reason.

In addition to dealing with the dog, it is vital to treat its surroundings also. The bed will need to be washed, powdered or sprayed as well as any bedding. The flea's life cycle takes about five weeks to complete, and the minute eggs are likely to be scattered around the floor. Any that escape into the environment are likely to hatch later, precipitating a new epidemic of scratching in your dog. Repeat treatments as directed.

In severe cases, you may need to call in a professional firm to treat your house so that no stages in the life cycle will remain viable. The chemicals used can have a residual action so that no other fleas will be able to establish themselves for a period of time. Do not forget to remove any other pets from the room such as fish that may be affected by chemical treatment, before the work starts. It is quite possible for dogs to transfer fleas to cats, and vice versa, so any felines in the house must also be treated. Bear in mind that they are likely to be even more susceptible to the effects of such chemicals than dogs.

PRECAUTIONS

As a precaution against fleas, some owners use flea collars for their pets, but these must be fitted strictly in accordance with the manufacturer's directions if they are to be effective and safe. If your dog has a naturally sensitive skin, check regularly to be sure there is no adverse reaction to the impregnated strip forming the collar.

Flea infestations build up during the summer months in temperate climates. Some owners prefer to bathe their dogs with an insecticidal shampoo to deter fleas and other external parasites. This should be mixed with a specified volume of water and is rinsed out of the coat. Other means of combating such parasites include pills and injections. The concentration of the drug in the blood kills the flea when it feeds but offers no protection to the dog's owner, who may also be bitten by these parasites. Thus, the environment must also be treated.

? ARE FLEAS HARMFUL TO DOGS?

Yes. Even in mild cases, their presence can cause not only scratching but also severe irritation which leads the dog to bite itself. In certain instances, dogs become allergic to the flea saliva which is injected in minute quantities when the flea bites. This results in a very bad reaction following a single contact with flea saliva. There are also various diseases and canine parasites that can be spread by fleas including the tapeworm *Dipylidium caninum*. Puppies that are bitten by fleas may suffer from anemia.

? WHAT ARE THE COMMON MITES THAT MAY AFFLICT MY DOG?

This will depend partly on the area where you live, but the mites described below are all relatively common on dogs. The skin irritation caused by any of these mites is described as mange, and it can prove difficult to treat successfully. The mite *Demodex canis* lives deep in the hair follicles and is usually associated with short-coated breeds, especially the dachshunds. It can cause hair loss, and thickening of the skin, and bacteria may invade the damaged tissue leading to the formation of pustules; the dog can become very sick. *Demodex* spreads from a bitch to her puppies although the symptoms may not be immediately apparent. Confirmation of the presence of *Demodex* requires skin scrapings viewed under the microscope to find the parasite. The condition is often difficult to treat. Infected bitches should not be mated to prevent the transmission of these mites to puppies.

Sarcoptes scabiei is found on the skin, and the first indication of its presence will probably be red patches on the inner surface of the thighs. The whole life cycle takes place on the dog and causes considerable irritation. Diagnosis is made the same way as *Demodex*, and treatment may have to be prolonged. If these mites are suspected, take precautions to see that they do not spread to humans, especially children. Another skin mite, which commonly afflicts puppies, is *Cheyletiella yasguri*. In older dogs in particular, this leads to an excessive build-up of scurf in the coat, which is in part the mites themselves, as they are white in color.

The ear mite, known as *Otodectes cynotis*, lives within the ears. These mites cause irritation by invading the sensitive tissue, and they will contribute to an existing infection. It is possible to see them *in situ* by means of an auroscope, but an accumulation of reddish-brown wax in the ear canal itself is indicative of their presence, especially if the dog paws repeatedly at its ears. Obtain treatment from your veterinarian.

Most species of mite normally live on the dog's body throughout their life cycle. The exception is the harvest mite *Trombicula autumnalis*. In this particular case, only the larval stage in the life cycle is likely to be parasitic. The adults appear as small, free-living spidery creatures, reddish in color. The larvae are found in vegetation and usually attach to the dog's paws between the pads and cause severe irritation. The dog will chew at its feet. A careful inspection will reveal the tiny groups of larvae responsible. The related North American chigger (*Eutrombicula alfreddugesi*) produces identical symptoms. Washing the feet by dipping them in a solution of insecticidal shampoo will kill the larvae.

Inspect your dog for fleas regularly (*above*), and as a preventative measure; it is a good idea to dust your dog at least twice a year with a reputable anti-parasitic dusting powder obtained from your veterinarian and dust the basket and bed at the same time. It also helps to use newspaper for bedding and burn it daily.

WHAT OTHER EXTERNAL PARASITES MAY AFFLICT MY DOG?

Lice are most likely to be seen on puppies; they are usually spread by direct contact or via grooming equipment. Typically, they congregate around the head where their egg-cases cling to individual hairs. In most instances, repeated treatment will be necessary to clear the infestation. Ticks, in comparison, live on dogs for only a short period in their life cycles, often dropping off after feeding on the dog's blood. Rather than pulling a tick out and possibly breaking off the head and leaving it embedded in the skin to act as the source of an infection, simply smear its body with petroleum jelly. With its respiratory pore blocked, the tick will be unable to breathe and will drop off intact.

In tropical areas especially, ticks can transmit serious blood-borne protozoal infections. One of the most widespread is *babesiosis*, the protozoan *Babesia canis* is linked to the brown dog tick *Rhipicephalus sanguineus*. The resulting illness is described as *redwater* because an acute anemia leads to reddish urine being produced. Blood transfusions as well as drugs are likely to be required if treatment is to be successful. Moving a dog to an area where such ticks are endemic carriers of babesiosis is hazardous, and the dog should be watched closely. The protozoa are easily detected in a blood smear, stained in an appropriate manner for microscopic examination.

Certain flies can also parasitize dogs. The flies are usually attracted to fecal deposits, where they lay their eggs. The eggs give rise to maggots which attack the skin and produce a toxin that enters the blood stream and can prove fatal. The fly larvae should be removed at the earliest opportunity and the affected area cleaned up, using antibiotics if necessary. In parts of the United States, dogs can be attacked by the maggots of the fly *Cuterebra maculata*. These invade the skin when the dog is walking over ground where the eggs from which the larvae hatch were originally laid. Thick-coated breeds are most likely to be attacked, and maggots will have to be removed by surgery.

Dietary methods can help to control external parasites. Large amounts of vitamin B generate an odor in the skin of dogs that is repellent to biting insects.

Mange can be very difficult to treat successfully, especially if, as in the case of *Demodex*, the mites are located deep within the hair follicles (*below*). This particular mite is typically associated with Dachshunds.

EXTERNAL PARASITES

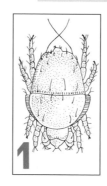
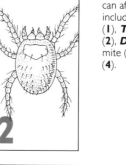

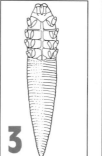
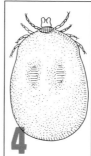

A variety of external parasites can afflict dogs and these include: **Cheyletiella**, fur mite (**1**), **Trombicula**, harvest mite (**2**), **Demodex**, demodectic mite (**3**), **Ixodes**, sheep tick (**4**).

INTERNAL PARASITES

Dealing with the majority of internal parasites is usually a straightforward procedure, since there are a number of effective drugs available. Internal parasites can be spread in several ways.

? HOW CAN I RECOGNIZE TAPEWORMS?

Tapeworms are named after their flattish appearance. They resemble a piece of whitish tape, becoming broader away from the head end. They anchor in the gut by their heads, and the segments of their bodies become mature towards the tail. Pieces break off and are passed out with feces. The segments are not directly infectious for other dogs however because they require an intermediate host. This, in the case of the tapeworm *Dipylidium caninum*, can be lice or fleas. The dog acquires the infection by consuming an external parasite that has been parasitized by the immature tapeworm. It may be possible to spot tapeworm segments around the dog's anus; they resemble rice grains in appearance and sometimes appear to move.

Other tapeworms use herbivores as intermediate hosts. Dogs acquire infection by eating raw meat containing the tapeworm cyst. One particular species, *Echinococcus granulosus*, is commonly associated with sheep, but can also be spread to humans. If a human ingests the eggs, cysts about 6 inches across may develop in the body with disastrous consequences. The adult tapeworm in this instance is remarkably small, attaining a maximum size of about one fifth of an inch, and does not cause obvious harm to the dog, even when there is a heavy burden present. In order to combat the risk posed by *Echinococcus*, the New Zealand government has made it compulsory to deworm dogs regularly, and this controls the problem effectively.

? ARE ROUNDWORMS IMPORTANT PARASITES IN THE DOG?

Considerable media attention has been focused on the slight but nevertheless real risk to human health posed by the canine roundworm known as *Toxocara canis*. Puppies are frequently born infected with this parasite, having acquired it from the bitch before birth. These roundworms may cause diarrhea, vomiting and a pot-bellied appearance. Repeated treatment through the pregnancy and following birth, as directed by a veterinarian, will eliminate the danger posed to human health. In fact, the eggs of *Toxocara canis*, when present in the feces, are not immediately infectious but must remain outside the body for some time before the larval stage can develop. Once primed, however, and ingested accidentally by a child, for example, the eggs will hatch in the gut and the larvae will migrate through the body, a process known as "*visceral larval migrans*." If the larvae develop in the eye, blindness can result. They may also invade the brain, with serious consequences.

HEARTWORM

Other roundworms may be more localized in their distribution. The heartworm (*Dirofilaria immitis*) occurs in the warmer parts of the world. It is transmitted when biting insects remove immature heartworms (called *microfilariae*) from the circulation of an infected animal and introduce them to another host when they feed again. The adult heartworm finally localizes in the blood vessels close to the heart making treatment very difficult. As a result, medication is given regularly to prevent the microfilariae from developing to the final stage in the life cycle, thus avoiding this problem.

LUNGWORM AND WHIPWORM

Dogs in kennels run the greatest risk of acquiring parasites, including certain roundworms. Coughing after exercise in the case of greyhounds suggests a lungworm (*Filaroides osleri*) infection. The parasites may be seen at the bifurcation of the trachea into the lungs with a fiber-optic endoscope. Whipworms (*Trichuris vulpis*) are also quite often encountered in greyhounds; they localize

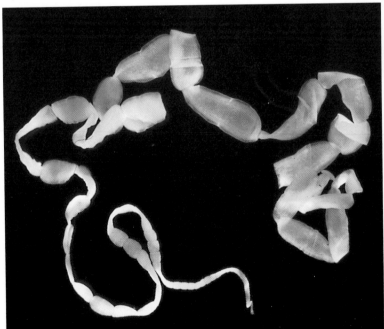

The dog tapeworm (*Dipylidium caninum, above*) uses the flea or louse as an intermediate host. It sheds eggs that pass out in feces and are eaten by fleas or lice. The dog infects or re-infects itself by eating the fleas or lice.

LIFE CYCLE OF THE ROUNDWORM

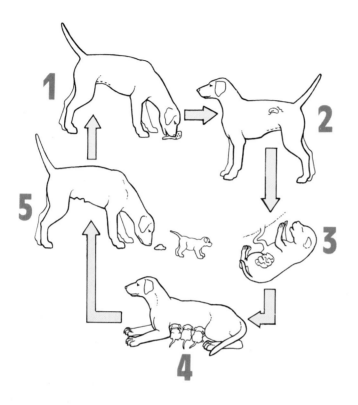

The embryonated infective eggs or larvae of the dog roundworm, *Toxocara canis* are ingested by the dog (**1**) and migrate to the body tissues (**2**) such as the kidneys. Unfortunately, the larvae usually enter the tissues of developing fetuses (**3**) and localize in their intestines, being activated by pregnancy. After the birth of the puppies the larvae can also migrate into the puppies' system and infect them through the mother's milk (**4**). The worms mature, passing eggs in the puppies' feces which are consumed by the mother and can reinfect her (**5**). Alternatively, larvae which fail to establish themselves and are passed out in the feces, may find another host and begin producing eggs. The eggs are not immediately infective, but need a short period outside the body to mature.

in the appendix and cause intermittent diarrhea.

Hookworms are also a danger in kennels because they enter the dog's body via its feet. Those of the *Ancylostoma* species then move to the intestines and may result in a severe anemia. Other hookworms such as *Uncinaria* tend to have less serious effects.

KIDNEY WORM

A rather peculiar nematode seen in certain parts of the world is the giant kidney worm *(Dioctophyma renale)*. It tends to localize in the right kidney in the majority of cases. The only treatment available is to remove the affected organ. This nematode is usually spread from raw fish, and females can grow up to 40 inches in total length. Although found in some parts of Europe, the kidney worm does not occur in the United Kingdom or Australia. It is endemic in parts of the United States and elsewhere. A dog will need rest after this treatment.

OTHER PARASITES

Various other parasitic worms can be spread to dogs, but they tend to be regional in distribution, especially if they are associated with the wildlife of an area. One parasite which resembles a worm in appearance, but is in fact a mite, is *Linguatula serrata*, popularly known as the tongue worm. It has a life cycle that requires an intermediate host such as a rabbit. A dog consuming the uncooked flesh of an infected herbivore can acquire these mites. They localize in the nasal chambers and cause a runny nose and impaired breathing. The dog may sneeze repeatedly, trying to dislodge the parasites, but they have to be removed by a veterinarian.

? **SHOULD I DEWORM MY DOG ON A REGULAR BASIS?**
Yes, this is vital, especially in a home with young children. Deworming is carried out against roundworms such as

Toxocara, which can be spread directly, as well as against tapeworms. Different medication may be required for the latter. Half-yearly dosing is recommended for adult dogs, but young puppies and dogs will need more frequent treatment. Treatment for tapeworms also requires control of the intermediate hosts when these are fleas or lice. In sheep farming areas, particular care is recommended because of the threat posed by the tapeworm disease *Hydatidosis*.

Check with your veterinarian on the recommended regimen for your area. It is probably preferable to obtain deworming pills from your veterinarian too, although products can be purchased elsewhere without prescription. If you do buy elsewhere, be sure to follow directions on dosage. The newer, less toxic compounds tend to be restricted to veterinary outlets, and you can be sure that you will receive sound advice and the correct medication for your dog there.

YOUR HEALTH AND YOUR DOG

As with all animals, there are diseases that the dog can spread to humans. Parasitic worm problems can be overcome by regular deworming.

? HOW SERIOUS IS THE THREAT POSED TO HUMAN HEALTH BY DOGS? HOW CAN I MINIMIZE THE RISKS?

Various diseases spread from dogs to humans, and these are termed *zoonoses*. In the vast majority of cases, there is no significant risk, especially if the dogs are dewormed regularly and their feces removed from the environment. Indeed, twice as many dogs are kept by families with children, and the benefits of ownership far outweigh the small, but significant, risk from zoonoses. Teach your children to wash their hands, especially if they have handled the dog prior to a meal time, and do not encourage a dog to lick their faces. If you or your family are bitten, clean the wound and see your doctor about inoculation. A dog bite may lead to tetanus; the bacteria are introduced via the deep puncture wounds caused by the canine teeth. The risk of rabies has been mentioned previously (see p.123).

The use of prepared or cooked food will minimize the threat of diseases such as salmonellosis affecting your dog and being transmitted to other members of the family.

There is potentially a much greater risk of zoonosic disease being acquired outside the home, since some dog owners are not fastidious about deworming. *Toxocara* eggs, for example, remain viable for a long time once established in the environment. The only means of destroying them is by intense heat on a hard surface such as concrete. In soil, they can survive for over two years. Stray dogs clearly represent a major source of infection, as they are less likely to have been regularly dewormed than a house pet. Children are most susceptible to *Toxocara* between the ages of eighteen months and three years, possibly because of their lifestyles. Try to supervise them when they are out in public places such as parks so they do not come into contact with feces. If regular deworming was required by law, as in New Zealand, the threat from *Toxocara* could be reduced even further; a move of this type would have the support of all concerned dog owners.

? WHAT IS RINGWORM, AND HOW CAN I RECOGNIZE IT ON MY DOG?

Ringworm is a fungal disease that affects the skin and hair; it is not a parasitic disorder as its name may suggest. Various fungi can lead to the characteristic circular bald patches with hair breaking off around the circumference of the site. The disease can often be confirmed by means of a Wood's light, which shows the fungus up as fluorescent green in a darkened room. Alternatively, cultures can be grown from skin scrapings, but the results may take several weeks as fungal growth can be slow, even in special cultural media. Specific antibiotic therapy using *griseofulvin* will be necessary, but this cannot be given safely to pregnant bitches for fear of causing fetal damage.

It is important to realize that the fungal spores will almost certainly have contaminated the dog's environment, especially its bed and grooming tools. If you have a cat in the house, have it tested as well because ringworm can be transmitted from dog to cat and vice versa, and the signs of infection are not generally as obvious in cats. Alcohol or disinfectants of the *iodoform* type are effective against spores, and every effort should be made to clean the environment thoroughly because ringworm is one of the diseases that can be spread from dogs to humans. If you develop reddish, circular lesions on your arms or elsewhere on your body, see your doctor.

Children are particularly vulnerable to some diseases, such as worms transmitted via the eggs of *Toxocara canis* in dogs' feces; therefore, children should be taught not to let dogs lick their faces and to wash their hands after touching a dog, before handling food.

FIRST AID PROCEDURES

The basic steps rely on commonsense, and are based on those techniques practiced on humans. There is always a risk that a dog may become involved in an accident, and the owner can help.

? HOW SHOULD I HANDLE A DOG THAT HAS BEEN INVOLVED IN A TRAFFIC ACCIDENT?

A dog that has been hit by a vehicle is likely to be in pain and distressed. Always approach it with caution because it may well bite. Rather than attempt to grasp the neck and attach a lead, restrain the dog by means of a noose. Loop the bottom of the lead through the handle, slip the noose over the head and then tighten, making sure that your hands are out of the dog's reach throughout. In an emergency, you may be able to use a belt in this way. Always try to catch the dog with minimum disturbance and avoid passing traffic yourself. Talk quietly to the dog and reassure it as far as possible. If it is very aggressive, a temporary muzzle may be required. Again, create a noose using a belt or tie. Loop it over the jaws, pull tight and knot the material behind the ears. Be sure that it is placed well back so it will not slip off accidentally. Muzzling short-nosed breeds can be particularly difficult.

When a dog is lying flat, move it very carefully because it may have serious internal injuries. And remember, it may attempt to snap. If there is a blanket available, gently transfer the dog to it, taking care not to tip it. With assistance, the dog can then be carried from the road in the blanket. Take the dog to a veterinarian immediately for a full examination.

? WHAT SHOULD I DO IF THE DOG IS BLEEDING BADLY?

You may not be aware of a serious internal hemorrhage, although the mucous membranes such as the gums will appear abnormally pale and the color will not return readily if the area is touched with a finger. The superficial scuffing and grazing often seen following a road traffic accident may be accompanied by bleeding, but this is usually self-limiting because the blood clots readily. If an artery has been severed, however, blood will spurt from the site of the injury. In this case your action may be vital in saving the dog's life. Wrap clean material around the apparent site of the hemorrhage and hold it tightly in place. This should help to stimulate the formation of a blood clot. Get someone to telephone the nearest veterinarian. Move the dog cautiously to minimize the blood loss. Tourniquets are dangerous if used for any length of time and should be avoided if possible.

A TEMPORARY MUZZLE

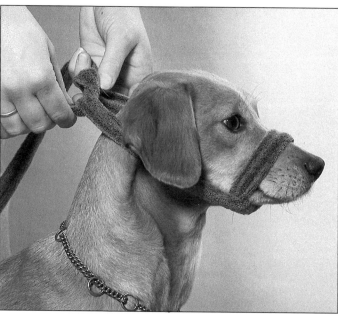

Rarely, as a form of restraint, an improvised muzzle, made of a length of bandage is useful. A loop is placed over both jaws, with the knot at the top of the nasal region. The free ends of the bandage are brought round under the jaw and then crossed and tied behind the ears.

There may be times, after a road accident for example, when it will be necessary to catch a stray dog. If it appears aggressive remember the possibility that it may be afflicted with rabies, and avoid touching it directly. Loop a belt or lead to form a noose and slip this over the dog's neck.

? WHAT ARE THE SIGNS OF SHOCK IN A DOG?

There are many causes of shock besides blood loss, including poisoning, fractures and burns. The symptoms are unmistakable. The dog becomes weak, and color disappears from the extremities. It appears cold, often shaking, and may be reluctant to stand. The heart beat is noticeably raised, while the respiratory rate tends to be shallow and rapid. Keep the dog warm (not excessively hot) and quiet and take whatever steps are necessary to counter the underlying cause of the symptoms of shock. If you have to take the dog to the veterinarian, wrap it carefully in a blanket and make it as comfortable as possible for the journey. Do not give alcohol because this is likely to prove counterproductive.

LIFTING AN INJURED DOG

Great care must be taken when moving an injured dog because it is likely to be in pain and may well attempt to bite, so avoid lifting or touching the dog more than necessary. If a blanket is available, use it as a temporary stretcher, and two people can hold it level by gripping the four corners.

? **IS IT POSSIBLE TO DISTINGUISH BETWEEN A FRACTURE AND A DISLOCATION? WHAT TREATMENT WILL BE NECESSARY?**

A fracture is a clear break in a bone, whereas a dislocation involves damage to a joint when one of the component bones is dislocated. In the case of a fracture, there will be no restraint on movement, but an audible grating sound *(crepitus)* is likely to accompany it. Avoid unnecessary handling as this will be painful for the dog. By way of contrast, a dislocation inhibits free movement. The swelling is confined to the region of the joint only, and the bone does not penetrate the skin.

The first aid you should provide is similar in either instance. Bearing in mind that the dog is in pain, try to restrain it. Confine it to a small area to encourage it to lie down and take the weight off the affected part of its body. Leave the treatment of the condition to the veterinarian. He may take X-rays to assess the state of the damage.

There is a congenital tendency in some breeds to develop *luxating patellae* (knee-caps). If the problem persists surgical correction may be necessary. In the case of a fracture, the veterinarian can opt to fix it internally by means of screws and plates for example or externally by placing the leg in a cast. The decision will depend on the site and type of fracture — cases where bone penetrates the skin are more serious than clean breaks.

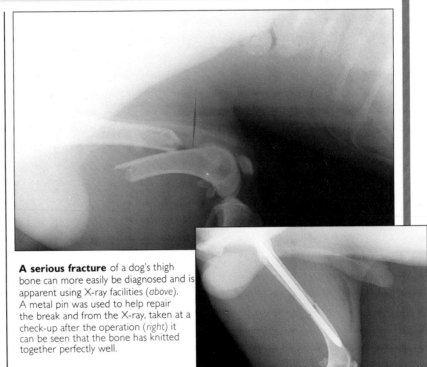

A serious fracture of a dog's thigh bone can more easily be diagnosed and is apparent using X-ray facilities (*above*). A metal pin was used to help repair the break and from the X-ray, taken at a check-up after the operation (*right*) it can be seen that the bone has knitted together perfectly well.

? **MY DOG HAS A GRASS SEED LODGED IN ITS PAW. WHAT CAN BE DONE TO REMOVE IT?**

Grass seeds are a relatively common "foreign body" that can injure a dog if they penetrate the skin. A sudden onset of lameness with the dog licking persistently at its paw may indicate the presence of a grass seed. If you can see the seed, pull it out with a pair of tweezers while someone else restrains the dog for you. Unfortunately, in many instances nothing will be visible because the grass seed will have tracked further up the leg. A veterinary examination using special forceps will be necessary. But even with these, it is not always possible to discover the seed responsible for the irritation.

Other foreign bodies such as glass, needles and pins can also be dangerous for your dog. Needles for example may be ingested accidentally and can become stuck in the mouth. Do not attempt to remove an object from the mouth yourself, if possible, because the tongue is a very vascular organ and profuse bleeding may result. The symptoms of the presence of a foreign body will depend very much on where the object has become lodged. Gagging and pawing at the face can be expected in this instance.

TREATING SHOCK

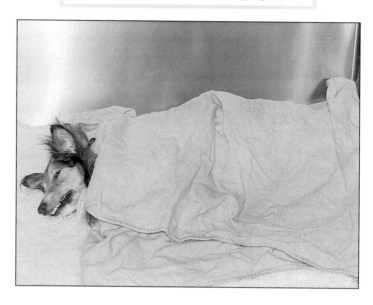

An accidental injury may give rise to shock and the response should be geared according to the particular problem. Keep the dog in a warm environment and seek professional advice.

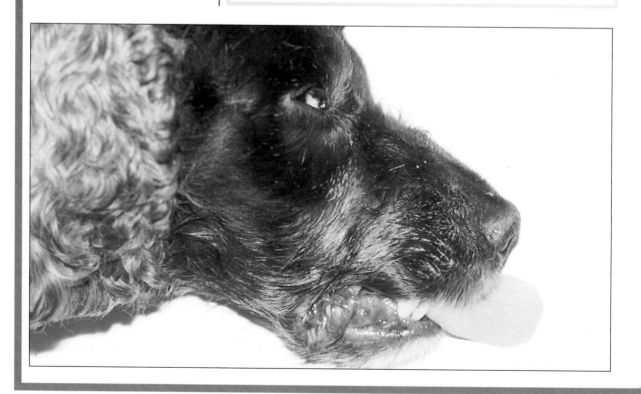

ARTIFICIAL RESPIRATION

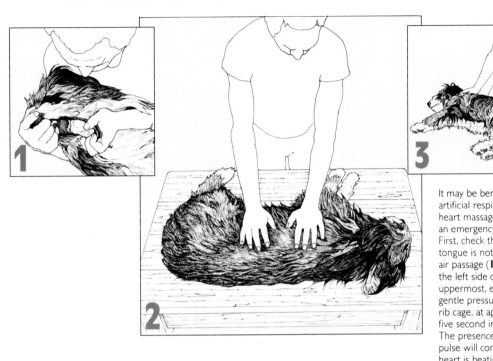

It may be beneficial to give artificial respiration and heart massage to a dog in an emergency situation. First, check that the tongue is not blocking the air passage (**1**), and with the left side of the body uppermost, exert firm but gentle pressure over the rib cage, at approximately five second intervals (**2**). The presence of a femoral pulse will confirm that the heart is beating (**3**).

An unconscious dog (*left*) needs immediate first aid treatment and the assistance of a veterinarian as soon as possible. All you can do is to insure that the tongue is pulled forward to prevent choking, keep the dog warm and it may help you to talk to him soothingly.

? **MY DOG COLLAPSED WHEN WE WERE COMING BACK FROM A WALK. HE DID RECOVER, BUT COULD IT HAPPEN AGAIN?**

This is an alarming situation, and you must seek veterinary advice. There could be a number of causes, and the problem could recur. Epilepsy is not unknown in dogs, especially Cocker Spaniels, and can lead to a sudden collapse. The dog appears to lose all control of its body functions during a seizure and may defecate as well as urinate. It will paddle with its legs while lying on its side. The cause is unknown, but treatment is available to control the seizures.

Another cause of collapse, especially in such brachycephalic breeds as the Bulldog, is a malformation in which the soft palate is longer than normal. This in turn may affect the larynx and prevent the dog from breathing normally at times. When this happens, pull the tongue forward at once and, if necessary, open the jaws to make sure there is no obstruction.

If there is no response, artificial respiration must be given without delay.

? **HOW SHOULD I TREAT MY DOG IF IT REQUIRES ARTIFICIAL RESPIRATION?**

If the dog is unable to breathe, the oxygen supply to the brain will be impaired, and the brain will be permanently damaged. In order to give artificial respiration, first make sure that the tongue does not block the entrance to the airway at the back of the mouth by pulling it forward. Then, with the dog on its right side, press gently and repeatedly on the rib cage with both hands at intervals of about five to ten seconds. If the chest wall has been punctured, by a deep wound for example, the usual pressure gradient will be lost, and you will have to adopt a different approach. Keeping the dog's jaws firmly closed, blow forcefully up the nostrils, with a few seconds gap between each breath. At the same time, check the heartbeat. Direct mouth to mouth resuscitation is of little value in the case of the dog.

Heatstroke is very dangerous because the only way dogs can control their body temperature is by panting (*above*) — causing heat loss from the body by evaporation of water — or through the pores between their toes and on the inside of the ears. Therefore it is vital for a dog to have access to a cool spot and plenty of water, particularly in hot climates.

To alleviate blood loss in an emergency, such as a cut paw pad which will bleed quite profusely, bind a bandage tightly around the foot before taking the dog to the veterinarian. It is advisable to carry the dog to prevent the weight being placed on the affected leg (*left*).

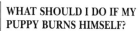

WHAT SHOULD I DO IF MY PUPPY BURNS HIMSELF?

Cool the burned area with cold water immediately to reduce the inflammation and then seek veterinary assistance. Burns, although superficial, may be serious and are likely to be slow to heal. Shock is inevitable, and a further complication may be bacterial infection.

WHAT SHOULD I DO IF MY PUPPY ELECTROCUTES HIMSELF?

Avoid this situation by never leaving an appliance plugged in and turned on in a room where there is a teething puppy that may choose to chew the wire. *Never* touch a dog that has been electrocuted until the source of the current has been switched off. This applies especially in the case of a dog on a railway line as it could prove fatal.

WE LIVE IN A HOT CLIMATE. SHOULD WE TAKE ANY SPECIAL CARE WITH OUR DOG?

Try to prevent your dog from going outside when the sun is at its hottest, particularly if there is any sign of reddening on its skin. This is likely to indicate sunburn and is especially common in the nasal region of collies and similar breeds. Repeated burning of sensitive areas can lead to skin cancer. To prevent burning, use a suitable barrier cream and darken the white areas with shoe polish if necessary.

It is not just dogs in cars that die from heatstroke. In hot weather, dogs in outdoor kennels or doghouses with poor ventilation can also die. If your dog is suffering from heatstroke, cool it down immediately with water until the rectal temperature is 1 °F above normal. The figure will fall to normal without further application of water. If it falls excessively, there is a danger that the dog may succumb to hypothermia. Have drinking water readily available, and massage the legs to improve the circulation at this critical time.

? HOW SHOULD I DEAL WITH INSECT AND SNAKE BITES?

Many young dogs are stung by insects such as wasps, usually on the head. In the case of a bee, the ruptured sting will be left behind and should be removed with tweezers. It will resemble a fine splinter partially protruding from the skin. The swelling will soon subside in most cases. If the dog was stung on its tongue, the tongue will become inflamed and may block the opening to the trachea making breathing difficult. Call your veterinarian if this should occur. Most dogs rapidly learn to distinguish stinging insects. But snakes can prove a different proposition. It will be useful if you can remember what the snake looked like even if you cannot identify it. Not all snakes are poisonous. However, in the United States there are several poisonous snakes such as the colorful coral snake and the rattlesnake, and two poisonous lizards and one species of poisonous toad. Deadly poisonous insects also occur in some parts of the world such as Australia. A close examination of a snake bite may help you to determine whether poison was released into the wound. If there is a large swelling with two holes in the center, it is likely that this was the case.

Often, a snake bite occurs when you are well away from a vehicle, and the availability of a veterinarian with anti-venom at hand is unlikely. If the bite is on the leg, tie a tourniquet around it to restrict the spread of the poison to the rest of the body. It should not be too tight; leave it loose enough so you can slip a finger under it when it is in place. An ice pack, created with ice cubes in a sock and applied to the site of the bite, will also be of assistance. Carry the dog if possible back to your vehicle and contact a veterinarian as soon as possible for further advice.

While it is feasible in dire emergencies to cut into the wound and suck out the poison, this is difficult in practice. Make a small cut between the two fang marks to reach the fluid, suck the wound and then spit the poison out. Finally, rinse your mouth out thoroughly.

? WHAT ARE THE MOST COMMON POISONS THAT DOGS ENCOUNTER?

Among common household products, there are poisonous substances that have a fatal attraction for dogs. Anti-freeze for example, contains *ethylene glycol*, which has a sweet flavor that dogs like. In the body, however, it converts to oxalic acid and is deadly poisonous, with only 1 ounce proving fatal for a dog of 15 pounds in weight. *Metaldehyde*, often combined with *arsenic* and used in slug baits, is also appealing to dogs and should be carefully monitored.

If diagnosed in time, it may be possible to reverse the effects, depending on the substance involved, but it is vital to give as much information as possible to your veterinarian. In certain instances, you may not realize that the dog has eaten poison. Certain preservatives and lead paint, for example, are likely to prove fatal if your dog chews woodwork. Some house plants and outdoor plants are poisonous too. The incidence of poisoning is higher in young dogs because of their natural curiosity and chewing instincts, and the risk is greatest for those which lack proper supervision. In case of emergency, call your local veterinary hospital or ask for information from the Poison Control Center.

There are no specialist medical items necessary for a dog's medical kit — bandages, plasters, cotton, gauze, antiseptic solution, eyewash and an eyedropper, tweezers to remove splinters, a mercury rectal thermometer, petroleum jelly, and possibly an emergency snakebite kit are sufficient.

THE POPULAR BREEDS

5

There is great diversity in the appearance of the various pedigreed breeds, and to a lesser extent, a wide range of temperaments. Some breeds remain scarce, and are likely to be expensive whereas others are often seen, with their asking price being a direct reflection of their pedigree. For those interested in showing their dogs, this factor becomes highly significant. It is generally accepted that there are over 300 distinct breeds of dog, although some of these are not recognized for show purposes, but have a long working tradition in their country of origin, and the dogs concerned are correspondingly similar in appearance.

The Puli (*right*) is a popular breed that was introduced to the United States in the 1920s but originated in Hungary as a Sheepdog as early as the seventeenth century.

POPULAR BREEDS

Every dog has his day and, as in other walks of life, there are changing interests in the dog world, and some breeds grow in numbers as others decline — merely according to the current whims of fashion.

? WHY IS THERE SUCH A VARIETY IN THE SIZE AND APPEARANCE OF DOGS?

This has come about as a result of selective breeding. It has been suggested that perhaps only 20 mutations such as shortened legs would have been necessary to give rise to the wide variety of dogs seen today. Approximately 4,000 generations of dogs have occurred since the start of domestication, and each generation increases the likelihood of mutations arising. Through selective breeding certain traits have been encouraged and in this way, the diversity of breeds seen today has arisen.

If two breeds with mismatching physical characteristics such as limb length, coat length and head shape are crossed, the offspring will be a mixture roughly halfway between the two parents. The explanation for this is that for some reason the mechanisms exist in most species to limit variations within the species, seem to have broken down. This has presumbably been caused by years of selective breeding for different types of dog.

Often, new characteristics have been developed simply for appearance and so the dog may well have been subject to greater selective breeding than any other domestic species, such as cows and cats in which comparable variations have not occurred.

Theoretically the species could become even more diverse. But recently, strict standards have been laid down for recognized breeds, with the predominant view that nature should not be stretched too far and that the variations existing today are quite sufficient.

Afghan Hound

Afghan Hound

Originating in the Middle East, these hounds are bred to hunt game and were valued for their coursing skills and great stamina. Afghans were introduced to the United Kingdom in 1907 and to the United States in 1927. It is currently a very popular breed because of its elegant appearance, but this tends to disguise its potential shortcomings. The long, silky coat needs considerable care, the active nature of these hounds can make training difficult, and they need regular periods of exercise.

Airedale Terrier

This breed originated in Yorkshire, England in the middle of the last century and has been popular as a working dog. It even saw active service during World War I. The largest of the terriers, the Airedale invariably makes a loyal household dog, remaining wary of strangers. It is not the easiest breed to show successfully, however, as its coat needs careful trimming.

Basenji

This breed evolved in central Africa, and the early stock imported to the United Kingdom proved very susceptible to distemper. It is probably of ancient lineage; dogs very similar in appearance to Basenjis occur on early Egyptian artefacts. The Basenji has unusual characteristics, including a modified laryngeal structure. This has given rise to its alternative name, "Barkless Dog," but this name is not entirely justified. The sleek appearance and friendly nature of the Basenji have contributed toward its popularity. These dogs may squabble among themselves in true pack dog fashion.

Basset Hound

The short-legged Basset Hound originated in France during the sixteenth century. It was used by hunters walking through the forests. Basset Hounds are friendly, but such is their determination to follow a scent that they may be reluctant to

Beagle

Bichon Frise

Bearded Collie

Borzoi

return to their owner when called. Adequate exercise is vital, if only to stop these hounds becoming overweight.

Beagle

Similar to the Basset Hound but with longer legs and shorter ears, the Beagle is apparently of British origin and was bred initially to hunt hares and rabbits, an activity which requires lengthy periods of exercise. Beagles are good-natured hounds as a general rule and are ideal family pets. But their willful side will be apparent at times. Short-legged breeds, such as these, may suffer from occasional back pains.

Bearded Collie

Essentially a working dog but also valued as a companion animal, the Bearded Collie has traditionally worked with sheep, especially in southern Scotland. Its coat needs regular, careful grooming to prevent matting. It may have an inherent

tendency to be attracted towards farm livestock when out in the country and thus needs to be watched accordingly.

Belgian Shepherd Dog

Four separate types of dog are grouped under this single heading. The Malinois is the only smooth-coated variety. The Groenendael is black in color overall. Both the Laekenois and the Tervueren resemble the Groenendael, but the Laekenois has a predominantly tan coat, which is rough, and the Tervueren is not as black as the Groenendael. The Belgian Shepherd Dog has been used for both herding and guarding purposes. It has an alert demeanor and is generally responsive to training.

Bichon Frise

This small breed was developed originally in the Mediterranean area and attracted the interest of nobility, but later it declined in popularity. It became a common circus

dog, learning various tricks readily. The Bichon Frise is a lively little dog of attractive appearance with a pure white coat.

Border Collie

Another Scottish herding breed and a frequent competitor at working dog trials. These dogs really do need to be kept in a working environment where they can use their skills and build up a rapport with their owner in this context.

Borzoi

This breed epitomizes all the qualities of the sight hounds with its elegant proportions and lithe movement. The Borzoi has been bred to chase prey by sight rather than by scent. It was developed in Russia in the thirteenth century. Borzois benefit from the opportunity to gallop regularly, and their coats need dedicated care if they are to remain in good condition.

Boston Terrier

Briard

Boxer

Bulldog

Boston Terrier
Developed from the mating of Bulldogs with Terriers, the Boston Terrier was named after the American city where it was bred during the last century. These dogs make good pets, but their relatively large heads, reflecting their Bulldog ancestry, can lead to obstetrical problems during whelping.

Boxer
Bred initially in Germany during the 1830s, the Boxer did not achieve any great degree of popularity for nearly a century. Today, they are well-known internationally. Both lively and intelligent, Boxers are perhaps not best suited to homes with young children because of their naturally exuberant temperaments, but they are not quarrelsome by nature.

Briard
A breed that has become increasingly popular during recent years, the Briard originated as long ago as the eighth century AD in France. They were kept initially for guarding stock from wolves, and then the herding side of their nature was developed. An intelligent and loyal dog, the Briard will need its coat groomed daily to maintain its attractive flowing appearance.

Brussels Griffon
A breed with enormous character, these dogs are derived from the Affenpinscher and other breeds including the Yorkshire Terrier. Responsive to most training, they may nevertheless resent the leash unless you start them on it early in life. The Brussels Griffon has a sensitive temperament and is usually shy in the company of strangers.

Bulldog
The traditional British breed, Bulldogs have changed considerably in appearance since they were first used in bull-baiting contests. Today, these dogs are docile by nature and in spite of various weaknesses, such as the wrinkled face which can predispose to infections, they have retained a high level of popularity. They rank among the more expensive breeds.

Bull Terrier
Both English and Staffordshire varieties have a stocky appearance and considerable courage, but other breeds are more suitable for homes with young children. Bull Terriers do not rank among the most placid of dogs, and white individuals are often deaf which can further handicap the training process.

Cavalier King Charles Spaniel
The Cavalier King Charles Spaniel has a more pronounced nose and a longer tail than the King Charles Spaniel and although they are very similar in appearance, they are recognized as separate breeds. They are vivacious as well

Chihuahua

Dalmatian

Chow

English Setter

as affectionate. As with all Spaniels, check their ears regularly for any signs of infection.

Chihuahua
A breed that originated in Mexico and was named after a state in that country, the Chihuahua was first seen in the United States in 1850. Both smooth and long-coated varieties exist. These small dogs are social by nature and capable of detecting any intruder. They bark quite loudly, at the earliest opportunity.

Chow
Introduced to the United Kingdom from China by seamen, the Chow is believed to be a very old Oriental breed. Unfortunately, in terms of temperament, these dogs tend to be difficult to train and rather snappy. Some individuals bite quite readily, but they can also be very affectionate. An unusual feature of the Chow is its bluish tongue.

Cocker Spaniel
Popular as a gundog and often seen in the show ring, the Cocker Spaniel can also settle well in the home. The smaller Cocker Spaniel is classified as a separate breed. It possesses a slightly longer coat, but is otherwise similar. Spaniels can usually be trained quite easily, although a few individuals may be rather neurotic. Ear infections are common in all Spaniels, and these breeds are no exception.

Dachshund
Various forms and sizes of Dachshunds are recognized; wire-haired, smooth-haired and long-haired breeds as well as miniature forms are known. They are from hound stock (bred from the German Teckel) and are courageous by nature. Their long bodies have made Dachshunds prone to spinal problems, and they are also afflicted with a relatively high incidence of *diabetes mellitus* — a disease which affects the sugar in the blood.

Dalmatian
The dappled appearance of the Dalmatian is not present at birth; puppies are born pure white and develop their circular and distinctive spots as they get older. These can be either brown or black. Dalmatians are easy dogs to care for and make useful guards. They can be prone to *urinary calculi*, due to a metabolic weakness.

Doberman Pinscher
Bred essentially as a protector of property, the Doberman is an alert and forceful dog that needs firm training from an early age. It is probably not the breed to have in a home with young children because some are excessively aggressive.

English Setter
The term "setter" comes from the work orginally undertaken by dogs of this type; having found game with their keen sense of smell, they sat (set) to indicate the location to their owner.

English Springer Spaniel

Great Dane

German Shepherd Dog

Hungarian Vizsla

English Springer Spaniel
A breed well-suited to hunting, these Spaniels will not only flush game but also retrieve it. They are loyal companions and may become particularly attached to their trainer. They can be reserved with strangers.

Flat-coated Retriever
Originally known as the Wavy-coated Retriever because of their resemblance to their Newfoundland ancestors, these dogs currently reveal the impact of Setters on their bloodline. A dependable breed either in the field or at home, they are probably best suited to rural areas in view of their active nature. In turn, these Retrievers have given rise to the Chesapeake Bay Retriever.

German Shepherd Dog
A very intelligent and popular breed, the German Shepherd can make an exceedingly trustworthy companion, but when challenged by a stranger these dogs are capable of revealing the determined and forceful side of their temperaments. Their characteristic prick-eared appearance may not be apparent until puppies are at least six months old. White individuals are generally frowned upon in exhibition circles, but they do not differ from the darker-colored siblings in temperament. In addition to *hip dysplasia*, the breed appears to be afflicted with a relatively high incidence of gastric problems which cause chronic diarrhea.

Golden Retriever
Bred initially in Scotland on Lord Tweedmouth's Guisachan estate, these dogs have gained a widespread following. About 5000 are being registered annually in the United States. Intelligent and gentle, Golden Retrievers are used both in police work, and as guide dogs for the blind. They make ideal companions, but be prepared to devote time to them.

Gordon Setter
Not seen as often as some other breeds of Setter, the Gordon has proved a loyal dog. They can run at a good gallop when necessary in the field and can be relied upon as retrievers because of their steady, phlegmatic temperaments.

Great Dane
These majestic dogs were developed in Germany and emerged as a recognizable breed during the last century. But their ancestry may be traced back directly to the large breeds of ancient Rome such as the Molossus. Their size necessitates that their surroundings be suitably spacious. These dogs are reluctant to take to strangers.

Greyhound
Track dogs of this breed are sometimes offered as family pets when their racing days are over. The settling-in period can be difficult, however, and great care must be taken when exercising such greyhounds.

Irish Setter

Keeshond

Irish Wolfhound

Labrador Retriever

They are capable of seizing small dogs, which doubtless remind them of the hare they chased but never caught. A proper muzzle may be necessary as a precaution at first. Greyhounds are also bred for show purposes, and, strangely, they do not suffer from *hip dysplasia*.

Hungarian Vizsla

A Hungarian breed combining the attributes of Retrievers and Pointers, the Vizsla has gained greatly in popularity both in Europe and the United States in recent years. Its lithe appearance and dependable, trustworthy temperament have contributed to its rise in popularity. Also, it is an elegant and superb gundog.

Irish Setter

Also popularly known as the Red Setter because of its deep chestnut coat, these dogs were originally red and white in color. Although they are not the easiest breed of Setter to train successfully, they make very

dependable gundogs and settle well in the home once the basic lessons have been learned. However, their temperaments may be too tense to fit in with children in a family.

Irish Wolfhound

A giant breed but one with a gentle disposition, the Irish Wolfhound is not suitable as a guard dog despite its awesome size. These hounds need a large area, and they may prove clumsy in the home. Puppies can be a liability until they are adequately trained.

Jack Russell Terrier

Not a recognized breed in the accepted sense, the Jack Russell is nevertheless widely owned. These dogs possess a true Terrier temperament but their appearance is somewhat different. They are avid rodent hunters when the opportunity presents itself. Certain individuals are highly-strung, but the

majority make lively companions.

Keeshond

The alternative name of Dutch Barge Dog belies the ancestry of this breed, which, for a period, was common sight on barges traveling the canals of Holland. It then went into decline, but now Keeshonden are seen with increasing frequency in the show ring and are gaining in popularity as pets. Their coats need regular grooming to look their best. Keeshonden make good watchdogs; they possess a characteristic bark reminscent of a ringing bell.

Labrador Retriever

This breed is popular both as a working dog and a household pet. Its intelligent and friendly temperament enhances its versatility, and Labrador Retrievers are also seen in large numbers at shows. They are generally trustworthy with children and detect the approach of strangers without difficulty.

Lhasa Apso

Pomeranian

Newfoundland

Pointer

Lhasa Apso

Introduced to the United States from its native Tibet during the 1930s, the Lhasa Apso has a lively nature coupled with considerable intelligence. Its long flowing coat must receive adequate care to maintain its overall appearance. The coat trails on the ground and tends to attract dirt and mud.

Newfoundland

Named after the country where the breed was developed, these dogs have a long nautical association. Not only were they involved in the rescue of drowning mariners, but they also assisted fishermen in their everyday tasks. A distinct variety, black and white in color, is known as the Landseer after the painter who portrayed such dogs in his work. The docile, amenable temperament of the Newfoundland is offset only by the breed's need for adequate exercise. This may not appeal to all potential owners.

Old English Sheepdog

These dogs were originally used for driving stock to market, but in recent years they have become extremely popular as pets, partly because of their appearances in films and on television. Unfortunately, many owners do not appreciate the need for lengthy grooming sessions and the breed's boisterous personality until they obtain one of these dogs. It is an appalling statistic that during 1982, over 1000 Old English Sheepdogs were given to the breed's rescue service. However, it is an obedient breed and friendly towards children.

Pekingese

Associated for centuries with the ruling Imperial family in China, the Pekingese was first smuggled out to the United Kingdom during 1860. Their small size belies a stubborn and aristocratic manner, and they can prove quite fearless. Care must be taken with their prominent eyes,

however; these are prone to injury, and if the dog is grasped too tightly by the scruff of its neck, they can be forced from their sockets.

Pointer

The Pointer was developed to detect game and reveal its location by pointing in its direction, and it has remained essentially a working dog. Various local varieties such as the Spanish Pointer have evolved, and all show the characteristic frozen posture adopted by a successful Pointer.

Pomeranian

The curled tail of these dogs reveals their Spitz ancestry, but they are really a toy variety of the powerful dogs used for pulling sleighs in the Arctic regions. Pomeranians have a lively disposition and are normally even-tempered, thus justifying their popularity as show and pet dogs. Be prepared for lengthy grooming sessions, because of their long coats.

Pyrenean Mountain Dog

Rottweiler

Rhodesian Ridgeback

Rough Collie

Poodle

Three distinct sizes of Poodle are recognized: the standard, the miniature and the toy, the smallest member of the group. Although now kept essentially as pets, the ancestors of Poodles were working dogs, adept in water. If you want to show your Poodle, check on the appropriate style of clipping required. This varies from one country to another. In terms of personality, these dogs are intelligent and responsive, although some toy Poodles may be highly-strung.

Pug

The almost pugnacious appearance of the Pug is not a true reflection of its personality, even though it is derived from mastiff stock. The black form is especially popular, and the short coat of the breed reduces the need for grooming to a bare minimum. Their squat faces can give rise to snuffling on occasions and their prominent eyes can be injured easily.

Pyrenean Mountain Dog

Known in the United States as the Great Pyrenees, these large dogs were bred originally to guard sheep against the ravages of wolves. They have retained their protective instincts, but in the United States, the breed's temperament has been considered suspect in recent years. Generally, however, these are loyal and diligent guard dogs, but their coats need regular attention.

Rhodesian Ridgeback

A breed developed specifically to cope with various adversities in Southern Africa ranging from ticks to drought, these dogs make obedient yet fearsome guard dogs. They were formerly kept for hunting lions and thus are not lacking in courage, but sound, early training is essential to prevent behavioral difficulties in later life. Their characteristic feature is a ridge, running down the spine, formed by a strip of hair growing in the opposite direction.

Rottweiler

Similar in temperament and requirements to the Rhodesian Ridgeback, the Rottweiler was first bred in Germany. After being used intially to guard cattle and drive them to market, the Rottweiler was then used in police work. The breed is named after the town of Rottweil in Southern Germany where it was first developed.

Rough Collie

Another Scottish sheepdog, the Rough Collie found favor with Queen Victoria and then a much wider audience despite the fact that it requires considerably more grooming than its smooth-coated counterpart. As working dogs, Collies have a natural intelligence and are highly responsive to their owners. There can be a problem in some bloodlines, however, with an inherited defect known as *collie eye anomaly* (CEA). This can be checked by a veterinarian.

St Bernard

Scottish Terrier

Saluki

Shetland Sheepdog

St Bernard

The tales of these dogs rescuing stranded travelers trapped by snow in the Alps are well known. They were said to have small flasks of brandy attached to their collars to revive people suffering from hypothermia, but the truth of the matter is unknown. The St Bernard is a large, powerful dog with a correspondingly large appetite. Some are afflicted with a weakness of their hind legs, but their temperament is invariably sound. Both rough and smooth-coated forms exist.

Saluki

An agile and fleet-footed breed developed in Africa, the Saluki pursued antelope and other game. It can be a useful guard dog on occasions, but like other sight hounds, it must have adequate exercise. The ancestors of the Saluki may have been known in the region of the River Nile as early as 329 BC. It is sometimes referred to as the Gazelle Hound.

Samoyed

These dogs were originally bred in the frozen wastelands of northern Siberia by Samoyed Indians to help herd reindeer. The Samoyed needed a versatile breed of dog, capable of controlling stock and of helping to move supplies on sledges through this inhospitable terrain. As a result, the breed today has a willing and friendly temperament and is very responsive to human company.

Scottish Terrier

Affectionately known as the "Scottie," this breed was originally known as the Aberdeen Terrier. It possesses typical Terrier characteristics including a willingness to hunt if a suitable opportunity presents itself and plenty of personality. They are normally rather aloof with strangers, and a few are bad-tempered. But adequate training from an early age should prevent such outbursts.

Shar-pei

This rare Chinese breed has attracted a great deal of attention in recent years. It nearly became extinct during the 1950s but has now been successfully revived through the efforts of a Hong Kong breeder, Matgo Low, with the help of dog fanciers' in the United States. In common with the Chow, the tongue of the Shar-pei is naturally bluish in color.

Shetland Sheepdog

Originating in the Shetland Islands off the north coast of Scotland, "Shelties" have gained an international following. They are obedient and responsive dogs, capable of great devotion to their owners, but they are shy with strangers. Their small size has also helped to insure their popularity, and their thick coats reflect the hardiness of this breed in adverse weather. They are easy to train since obedience was instilled into the breed, early in its development in the early 1900s.

Shih Tzu

Welsh Corgi

Weimaraner

West Highland White Terrier

Shih Tzu

The name of these small dogs means "lion" and refers to their similarity in appearance to these big cats. The Shih Tzu was a highly valued breed during the Chinese Ming dynasty (1368-1628) and finally reached the United States during the 1940s.. They are relatively easy to show and make good house dogs, reveling in attention.

Weimaraner

The early development of the Weimaraner was rigorously controlled in Germany, and demand for this superior gundog usually exceeded supply in the formative years. Today, Weimaraners are more widely distributed. The breed is both obedient and loyal and requires little grooming to maintain its sleek appearance. The breed was developed during the mid-seventeenth century by the Dukes of Saxony and Weimar which led to their characteristic, unique solid, silver-grey coat color.

Welsh Corgi

There are two varieties, and they are named after the old Welsh counties where they originated. The Cardigan has a significantly longer tail than its Pembroke counterpart and rounded rather than pointed ears. The Pembroke has received considerable publicity because it is owned by the British Royal Family, and it is seen most often. But it tends to be more excitable than the Cardigan Welsh Corgi. Both varieties make good guard dogs and are usually obedient. But some individuals have a tendency to nip if provoked.

West Highland White Terrier

Believed to have been first bred in Scotland during the 1880s, "Westies" are lively Terriers with somewhat independent natures. They must receive adequate training early in life. They can prove very affectionate, however, and are both bold and alert. Their coats must be adequately groomed if they are to look their best.

They were bred to hunt small animals and often used to hunt vermin. Initially these Terriers were considered as a variety of the Scottish Terrier, but were subjected to a strict breeding program to establish distinctive characteristics.

Whippet

A fast breed originating in the industrial heartland of nineteenth-century England, the Whippet was developed to participate in the sport of dog racing. It is not outpaced by any other breed, including the Greyhound, and can cover 200 yards in under 12 seconds. As pets, these dogs have much in their favor. They are trustworthy with children, easy to groom and require little exercise, except a good gallop.

Yorkshire Terrier

Developed in the county of Yorkshire, England, from larger stock, these Terriers now rank among the most popular of the toy breeds.

GLOSSARY

Apple-headed The high, domed shape of the skull, notably associated with Chihuahuas.

Apron The longer hair which forms a frill at the base of the neck in certain breeds such as Rough Collies.

Bat ears Broad ears, with rounded appearance like those of a bat. A feature of the French Bulldog.

Beard Thick, long hair on the lower jaw of dogs such as the Brussels Griffon.

Benched The term used to describe a show dog in its official resting area.

Bite The relative positions of the upper and lower jaws when the mouth is closed.

Blaze Thin white stripe on the forehead, typically dividing the eyes.

Bloom The gloss on the coat of a healthy dog.

Blue merle A mix of blue and grey hairs in a black coat, resembling marble in overall color.

Bobtail A dog typically lacking a tail. Associated with the Old English Sheepdog.

Bone The appearance of the legs. A well-boned dog has a sound and powerful gait.

Bossy Excessively muscular shoulders, typically associated with the French Bulldog.

Brindle A coat with dark and light hairs, such as black and brown.

Brisket The underpart of the chest beneath the forelegs.

Broken Irregular patterning.

Brood bitch Breeding female.

Brush Thick tail, resembling that of a fox.

Burr Inner part of the ear.

Butterfly nose Blackish nose, with pinkish areas.

Button ears Vertical ears that fall forward at their tips.

Canid Belonging to the genus Canis. Includes domestic dogs.

Canines Sharp and long teeth situated at the corners of both jaws.

Castration Neutering of a male dog.

China eye A clear blue eye.

Check chain A chain which when fitted correctly should assist with training, discouraging the dog from pulling ahead or lagging behind when walking on a leash (also referred to as a choke chain).

Chops The folds of skin or jowls on the upper jaw, which are especially pronounced in some breeds, such as the Bulldog.

Clip The trimming of the coat, especially significant in poodles.

Coarse A dog with poor show potential.

Cobby Short and thick-set appearance.

Collar A means of controlling a dog, or, white markings also around the neck.

Couplings The part of the body extending from the last rib to the hip on each side, which can be variable in length.

Coursing The hunting of game by sight hounds. Can be organized as hare coursing.

Crank tail Low carriage of the tail.

Crest The highest part of the neck. Also specifically, the area of hair present on the head of a Chinese Crested Dog.

Cropping A surgical procedure which keeps the ears erect in dogs such as Boxers. It is said to create a more fearsome appearance but is outlawed in many areas.

Cross-bred Essentially a first-generation cross, between two pure, yet different breeds.

Croup The rear end of the body.

Crown The highest point of the skull.

Cryptorchidism Absence of one or both testicles from the scrotal sac, being described as unilateral or bilateral respectively.

Culotte The longer hair on the back of thighs of breeds such as the Pomeranian.

Cur Mongrel.

Cushion A thickening of the upper lips, seen in breeds such as Bulldogs.

Dam Female parent.

Dapple mottling No single dominant color in the coat.

Dew claw Vestigial digits terminating in claws, found on the inside of the legs, slightly off the ground. Often removed by surgery to prevent injury.

Dewlap Pendulous skin beneath the throat.

Dock Remove all or part of a young puppy's tail.

Dog Notably the male.

Drop ears Pendulous ears which lay close to the head.

Ectropion Eyelids directed abnormally away from the eye.

Entropion Eyelids directed abnormally inwards towards the eye.

Expression The facial appearance.

Eye teeth Canines in the upper jaw.

Fall Hair obscuring the facial features.

Feathering The fine long areas of hair, at the back of the legs and ears, especially apparent in Setters.

Flag A long tail or flowing hair around the tail.

Flanks Sides of the body from the end of the ribs to the hips.

Flews Pendulous top lips.

Furrow area Runs from the center of the skull to the top of the nose.

Grizzled Bluish-gray coloration.

Guard hairs Longer hairs hiding a shorter undercoat.

Gun-barrel front Very straight forelegs.

Hackles The hairs on the neck and back that are raised when the dog is under threat.

Hard-mouthed A Retriever which marks game with its teeth.

Harlequin Dark patches, normally blue or black, offset against white areas, typically associated with the Great Dane.

Harsh coat Wiry, or possibly in poor condition.

Heat The bitch's period of reproductive activity.

Hocks Heel joints, between stifle and pastern joints.

Inbreeding The mating of very closely-related stock, such as sire to daughter.

Incisors The teeth between the canines at the front of the mouth.

Jowls The pronounced fleshy area of the lips associated with some breeds such as the Bulldog.

Kiss marks Small spotted areas on the face, usually brownish in color.

Leathers The ear flaps.

Line-breeding Mating of more distantly-related stock than is seen with inbreeding.

Litter The puppies born in a single whelping.

Liver Dark reddish-brown.

Milk teeth The first, deciduous set of teeth.

Muzzle The area below the eyes on the face. Also a means of restraining a dog so that it cannot bite.

Occiput The rear high point of the skull.

Outcross The use of a totally unrelated dog or bitch for breeding purposes within a stud.

Overshot Protruding upper jaw, causing upper incisors to extend past the lower ones.

Pads Tough yet vascular areas on the feet which are devoid of hair.

Particolored Two colors with even distribution in the coat.

Patern Foreleg extending between the carpus and digits.

Pedigree The ancestry of a pure bred dog over several generations.

Points The color on the extremities of the body.

Prefix The kennel name which precedes the dog's individual name for the purpose of its official pedigreed name.

Premolars Teeth between the molars and canines.

Pricked ears Carried erect, but can show pointed tips.

Roached back A curved back, as seen in the Whippet.

Roan White and colored hairs mixed together, as is seen in Cocker Spaniels.

Rose ear A small ear which is folded to reveal the inner surface or burr.

Ruff The characteristic area of long hair around the neck of the Chow.

Sable Typically gold mixed with dark black hair, as in the Shetland Sheepdog.

Saddle Black marking extending over the back.

Screw tail Short and twisted tail.

Season The active reproductive phase of the bitch's cycle.

Self-colored Single-colored.

Spay Surgical neutering of a bitch.

Splay foot Toes kept wide apart.

Standard The features of the various breeds, as laid down by the governing authority concerned.

Staring coat A sign of poor condition.

Stern Tail of a hound or other sporting dog.

Stifle Hindlimb joint between upper and lower thighs.

Stop The slight indentation where the nasal bones fuse with the skull.

Top knot The tuft of hair at the top of the skull.

Tricolor Three colors, normally black, tan and white in approximately equal proportions on the coat.

Tuck up Sharp curvature in the stomach region, associated with Greyhounds and similar broad-chested breeds.

Undershot Lower jaw and incisor teeth protrude past the upper jaw when the jaws are closed.

Wall eye Iris is whitish or bluish in coloration. Only one eye may be affected.

Whelping Giving birth.

Wire-haired Rough-coated.

Withers Highest point of the shoulders, from where the dog's height is measured.

INDEX

Page numbers in *italic* refer to the illustrations and captions.

ACKNOWLEDGMENTS

The publishers acknowledge the cooperation of photographers, photographic agencies and organizations listed below.
Abbreviations used are: t top; c center; b bottom; l left; r right; u upper; lw lower.

8 Hazel Edington; 6 (c) Ardea, London; (b) David Alderton; 7 Ardea, London; 11 Sally Anne Thompson; 12 Sally Anne Thompson; 13 Marc Henrie; 14-15 Sally Anne Thompson; 16-17 Sally Anne Thompson; 18 Ardea, London (Jean Paul Ferrero); 19 Marc Henrie; 22-23 Sally Anne Thompson; 26 Sally Anne Thompson; 28-29 Marc Henrie; 31 Marc Henrie; 32 Bradley Viner; 33 Marc Henrie; 34-35 Sally Anne Thompson; 37 Ardea, London; 38 (t) Spectrum Colour Library; (b) Hazel Edington; 40-41 Marc Henrie; 44-45 Sally Anne Thompson; 46 Sally Anne Thompson; 47 Hazel Edington; 48 (t) Sally Anne Thompson; (cl) Marc Henrie; 49 Bradley Viner; 50 Ardea, London; 51 R. Willbie; 53 Sally Anne Thompson; 54 Marc Henrie; 56 Sally Anne Thompson; 58 Sally Anne Thompson; 59 (t) Ardea, London (c) Marc Henrie; 61 (t) Marc Henrie; (b) Hazel Edington; 63 (t) Sally Anne Thompson; (b) Peter Clark; 64 Hazel Edington; 65 Sally Anne Thompson; 67 (l) Ardea, London; (r) Sally Anne Thompson; 68 (t) Marc Henrie; (b) Ardea, London; 69 (c) Ardea, London; (b) Marc Henrie; 70 Ardea, London; 71 (t) Sally Anne Thompson; (b) Ardea, London; 72 Sally Anne Thompson; 73 Hazel Edington; 74-75 Ardea, London; 76 Ardea, London; 77 Marc Henrie; 79 Spectrum Colour Library; 80 Sally Anne Thompson; 84 Sally Anne Thompson; 86 Marc Henrie; 89 Marc Henrie; 90 Sally Anne Thompson; 91 (t) Marc Henrie; (c) Sally Anne Thompson; 93 Marc Henrie; 95 Spectrum Colour Library; 96 Marc Henrie; 97 Sally Anne Thompson; 101 Sally Anne Thompson; 102 Bradley Viner; 103 David Alderton; 104 Sally Anne Thompson; 105 Peter Clark; 107 Sally Anne Thompson; 108 Peter Clark; 109 Hazel Edington; 110-111 Sally Anne Thompson; 113 Sally Anne Thompson; 114 (t) Sally Anne Thompson; (c) Marc Henrie; (b) Bradley Viner; 115 Bradley Viner; 116-117 Marc Henrie; 118 Peter Clark; 119 (t) Bradley Viner; (b) Peter Clark; 120 Science Photo Library; 122 Peter Clark; 125 Marc Henrie; 126-127 Peter Clark; 128 Peter Clark; 129 Bradley Viner; 131 Hazel Edington; 132 Bradley Viner; 133 Glaxo; 135 David Alderton; 136 Sally Anne Thompson; 137 (t) Sally Anne Thompson; (c and b) Peter Clark; 138 Bradley Viner; 140 (c) Spectrum Colour Library; 140-141 Sally Anne Thompson; 143 Ardea, London (Jean Paul Ferrero); 144-153 Sally Anne Thompson.

All other photographs, property of Quarto Publishing Limited.